Cambridge Elements

Elements in Metaphysics
edited by
Tuomas E. Tahko
University of Bristol

THE METAPHYSICS OF COLOR

Michael Watkins
Auburn University

Elay Shech
Auburn University

Shaftesbury Road, Cambridge CB2 8EA, United Kingdom

One Liberty Plaza, 20th Floor, New York, NY 10006, USA

477 Williamstown Road, Port Melbourne, VIC 3207, Australia

314–321, 3rd Floor, Plot 3, Splendor Forum, Jasola District Centre, New Delhi – 110025, India

103 Penang Road, #05-06/07, Visioncrest Commercial, Singapore 238467

Cambridge University Press is part of Cambridge University Press & Assessment, a department of the University of Cambridge.

We share the University's mission to contribute to society through the pursuit of education, learning and research at the highest international levels of excellence.

www.cambridge.org
Information on this title: www.cambridge.org/9781009494441
DOI: 10.1017/9781009324212

© Michael Watkins and Elay Shech 2025

This publication is in copyright. Subject to statutory exception and to the provisions of relevant collective licensing agreements, with the exception of the Creative Commons version the link for which is provided below, no reproduction of any part may take place without the written permission of Cambridge University Press & Assessment.

An online version of this work is published at doi.org/10.1017/9781009324212 under a Creative Commons Open Access license CC-BY-NC 4.0 which permits re-use, distribution and reproduction in any medium for non-commercial purposes providing appropriate credit to the original work is given and any changes made are indicated. To view a copy of this license visit https://creativecommons.org/licenses/by-nc/4.0

When citing this work, please include a reference to the DOI 10.1017/9781009324212

First published 2025

A catalogue record for this publication is available from the British Library

ISBN 978-1-009-49444-1 Hardback
ISBN 978-1-009-32424-3 Paperback
ISSN 2633-9862 (online)
ISSN 2633-9854 (print)

Cambridge University Press & Assessment has no responsibility for the persistence or accuracy of URLs for external or third-party internet websites referred to in this publication and does not guarantee that any content on such websites is, or will remain, accurate or appropriate.

For EU product safety concerns, contact us at Calle de José Abascal, 56, 1°, 28003 Madrid, Spain, or email eugpsr@cambridge.org

The Metaphysics of Color

Elements in Metaphysics

DOI: 10.1017/9781009324212
First published online: March 2025

Michael Watkins
Auburn University

Elay Shech
Auburn University

Author for correspondence: Michael Watkins, watkigm@auburn.edu

Abstract: This Element offers an opinionated and selective introduction to philosophical issues concerning the metaphysics of color. The opinion defended is that colors are objective features of our world; objects are colored, and they have those colors independent of how they are experienced. It is a minority opinion. Many philosophers thinking about color experience argue that perceptual variation, the fact that color experiences vary from observer to observer and from viewing condition to viewing condition, makes objectivism untenable. Many philosophers thinking about colors and science argue that colors are ontologically unnecessary; nothing to be explained requires an appeal to colors. A careful look at arguments from perceptual variation shows that those arguments are not compelling, and especially once it is clear how to individuate colors. Moreover, a careful look at scientific explanations shows that colors are explanatorily essential. This title is also available as Open Access on Cambridge Core.

This Element also has a video abstract: www.cambridge.org/EMPH_Watkins

Keywords: color, realism, realization, perceptual variation, objectivism

© Michael Watkins and Elay Shech 2025

ISBNs: 9781009494441 (HB), 9781009324243 (PB), 9781009324212 (OC)
ISSNs: 2633-9862 (online), 2633-9854 (print)

Contents

1 Into the Rabbit Hole: Why Colors seem so Challenging   1

2 A Brief History of the Problem and Possible Solutions   13

3 Out of the Rabbit Hole   22

4 Reweaving the Rainbow   35

5 Realism in the Metaphysics of Science   50

6 Conclusion   67

   References   69

1 Into the Rabbit Hole: Why Colors seem so Challenging

1.1 Colors and Color Perception

Much of our knowledge of the world is perceptual. Even if you have never seen a giraffe, even if you have never seen a photo of a giraffe, it is only because many have seen giraffes that you know that giraffes exist. Of course, skeptics lurk. Can we tell the difference between a genuine perception and an illusion? If we cannot, then how do we know that we see anything? And if we do not know that, then how can we know anything of the external world?

This much, however, we can all accept: if we have knowledge of the external world, then that knowledge depends on perception. And if we have knowledge of the colors of objects, then that knowledge surely depends on perception. Indeed, were we to conclude that we have no perceptual knowledge of colors, then we would surely conclude that we have no reason to believe that anything is colored.

We describe the world we see as colored. We choose a paint for our room for its color. We might decide on one car over another because of its color. Many of us have our favorite colors. And all of this – the describing, choosing, deciding, and favoring just mentioned – is based partly on how the world visually appears to us. We know by perception that objects are colored, if we know it at all.

Again, skeptics lurk. But here we put aside general skeptical worries. Those are for another time and place. Those worries properly concern epistemology. Our concerns are metaphysical: Are objects colored and, if objects are colored, do objects have their colors independent of how they appear to observers? Put another way: Are colors real and, if they are, are they objective features of the world? We will assume, as everyone does much of the time, that we have knowledge of the external world, and that much of that knowledge is perceptual. Of course, putting aside general skeptical worries is not to put aside skeptical worries about colors. Indeed, skeptical worries about colors are often motivated by perception, or, more specifically, by perceptual variation. We don't see the colors of objects the same way, and each of us will sometimes see the color of an object differently depending on the lighting or the background against which we see the object.

Now just how perceptual variation challenges the thought that objects are colored might seem obvious, but we think it is less obvious than it might seem. Before turning to that we want to look at a way of thinking about colors that has been very influential and that, we suspect, helps to motivate worries about perceptual variation.

1.2 Color Space

Every color, we might think, has a particular hue, saturation, and brightness. Given that thought, we might think that every color can be represented on a three-dimensional color chart (see Figure 1).[1]

If we think of each color as essentially having some hue, brightness, and saturation, we can think of each color as being uniquely located on the chart. It will have some hue, and so some location around the sphere; that hue will be more or less saturated, and so some location between the center of the sphere (if it is less saturated) and the surface of the sphere (if it is more saturated); and it will have some amount of brightness, and so some location from the top of the sphere (for those shades that are brighter) to the bottom (for those that are darker).

Here's a way to think about how such a color space might be created. Imagine that you have three blue cards: O_1, O_2, and O_3. O_1 and O_2 are indiscernible in color; O_2, and O_3 are indiscernible in color; but O_1 and O_3 are discernible in color. Let's imagine that O_3 appears slightly more reddish than O_1. Wherever we place O_1, then, O_2 will be to the redward side of O_1, and O_3 to the redward

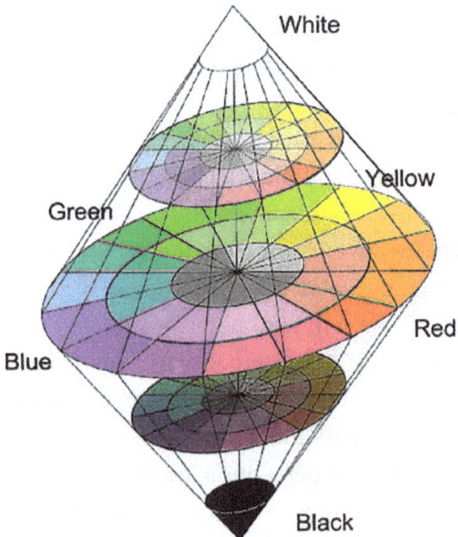

Figure 1 The Munsell color chart. From *The Encyclopedia Britannica* (www.britannica.com/science/Munsell-color-system).

---

[1] For discussions of the various ways in which color space might be represented and constructed, see Jan Koenderink and Andrea van Doorn (2003), Daina Raffman (2015), David Briggs (2021), and Mohan Matthen (2021).

side of O_2. Likewise, if the perceived difference is a difference in brightness or saturation, then the ordering would go up or down, or inward or outward.

If we think of colors this way, as each color essentially having some hue, saturation, and brightness, then we might think that for something to have a particular color is for that color to have a particular location in color space. And so, it might seem, if we cannot determine where in color space any object's color is located, then we cannot determine any object's color. One way we might think about the problem of perceptual variation, then, is that perceptual variation makes it impossible to non-arbitrarily determine the colors of objects because it makes it impossible to determine exactly where in color space some object's color belongs. And if we cannot determine the colors of objects, something we thought we could do merely by looking, then why think that anything is colored? Now let's see how perceptual variation seemingly makes such placement impossible.

1.3 Perceptual Variation

Perceptual variation might result for an observer due to different backgrounds or different lighting conditions. For instance, in Figure 2, most observers will report that the square on the left appears darker than the one on the right, even though the squares are alike in how they reflect light and even though they would appear to be the same color were they placed side by side against the same background. And although generally an object will appear roughly the same color across a range of lighting conditions due to a phenomenon known as color constancy, changes in lighting conditions, even changes in daylight, will at times bring about stark changes in the ways that colors appear.[2] This will be especially true of objects matching metamerically, that is, objects that appear the same in color under some lighting condition to some observers despite having different reflectance profiles, as in Figure 3.[3] Put another way, objects that match metamerically look the same in color under certain lighting conditions and to some observers even though the light reflected from their surfaces are not the same wavelengths and may be very different.

Variation between observers is also remarkable. If we offer a group of observers a set of color chips ordered from greenish blue to blueish red and ask each subject to choose that chip that is unique blue (i.e., that chip that is blue with no green or red in it), there will be a surprisingly wide range of responses, even amongst

---

[2] See Derek Brown (2021) for a recent discussion of the philosophical importance of color constancy. Also see Joshua Gert (2010 and 2017), Derek Brown (2014), Mazvitta Chirimuuta (2008), Jonathan Cohen (2008), David Hilbert (2005 and 2011), and Mark Eli Kalderon (2008).
[3] By "reflectance profiles" we mean "the capacity to differentially reflect wavelengths from different regions of the incident illumination" (Barry Maund 2022).

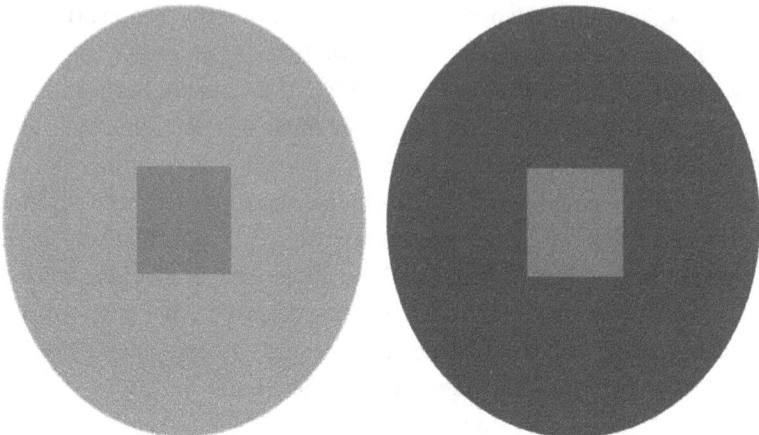

Figure 2 Identical squares and different backgrounds. The two center gray squares have equal reflectances, but the one against the lighter background appears darker than the one against the darker background.

seemingly normal observers.[4] This is partly explained by the fact that there is considerable intersubjective variation between the sensitivities of the cones had by seemingly normal human observers. So, what appears unique blue to me will likely appear at least somewhat reddish or greenish to you.[5] It is also estimated that about 12 percent of women are tetrachromats, having four cone types. (Although only a small percentage of these women see more colors than the rest of us.)[6]

When we move from humans to other animals, perceptual variation is even more striking. Normal human observers have three cone types, each type responding differently to light of different wavelengths. Moreover, color vision does not result only from how those cones respond; the outputs of those cones are then processed. Human color vision not only involves the eye, but the brain as well. One influential theory has it that those cones are functionally organized into two chromatic opponent systems: the red–green system and the yellow–blue system.[7] And so when the red–green system

---

[4] Hurvich, Jameson, and Cohen (1968).
[5] The range is surprisingly large, and especially for unique green. See Rolf Kuehni (2004). Kuehni takes this as evidence that colors are not objective features of the world. Interestingly, this judgment comes just after Kuehni offers this explanation for why there is so much variation with respect to unique green: "the pervasive nature of green in the natural environment of many people ... may offer an explanation for the large variability in UG (162)". In Section 5, we discuss roles the colors play in various scientific explanations and what that suggests about the ontology of colors.
[6] Deleniv (2015).
[7] The theory was first proposed by Ewald Hering (1964) in 1920. For philosophically informed discussions of the theory and its development, see C. L. Hardin (1988) and Raffman (2015).

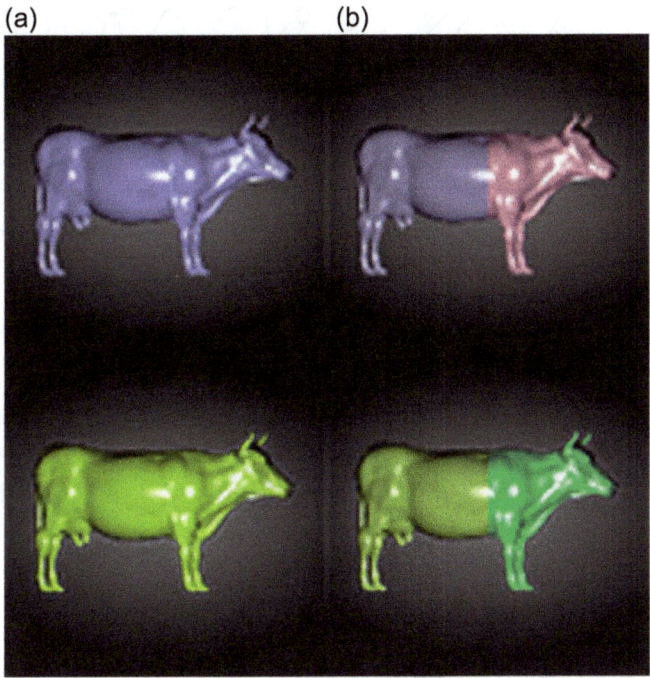

Figure 3 Metacows. The image on the (a) above was rendered under illuminant A with the CIE 2 degree observer, and then converted to display sRGB using the CIECAT02 chromatic adaptation transform. The image on the (b) was rendered under D65 with actual digital camera spectral sensitivities. From www.rit.edu/cos/colorscience/rc_db_metacow.php.

responds positively, the experience is reddish; when it responds negatively, the experience is greenish. A pure red experience, an experience of unique red, occurs when the red–green system responds positively, and the yellow–blue system is neutral. But most animals have more or fewer cone types, and they may be organized in different ways. Most nonhuman mammals have two. Many birds and fish have four. Mantis shrimp have between twelve and sixteen. The color space for other animals must differ widely from ours. But even animals with the same number of cone types will often experience different colors, or experience colors very differently (see Figure 4). Honeybees, like humans, have three cone types, but the visual system of honeybees is sensitive to ultraviolet light and is not sensitive to light in the red range (between 620 and 700 nm). Consequently, a flower that looks uniformly yellow to us will appear to have two colors to the bee if, for

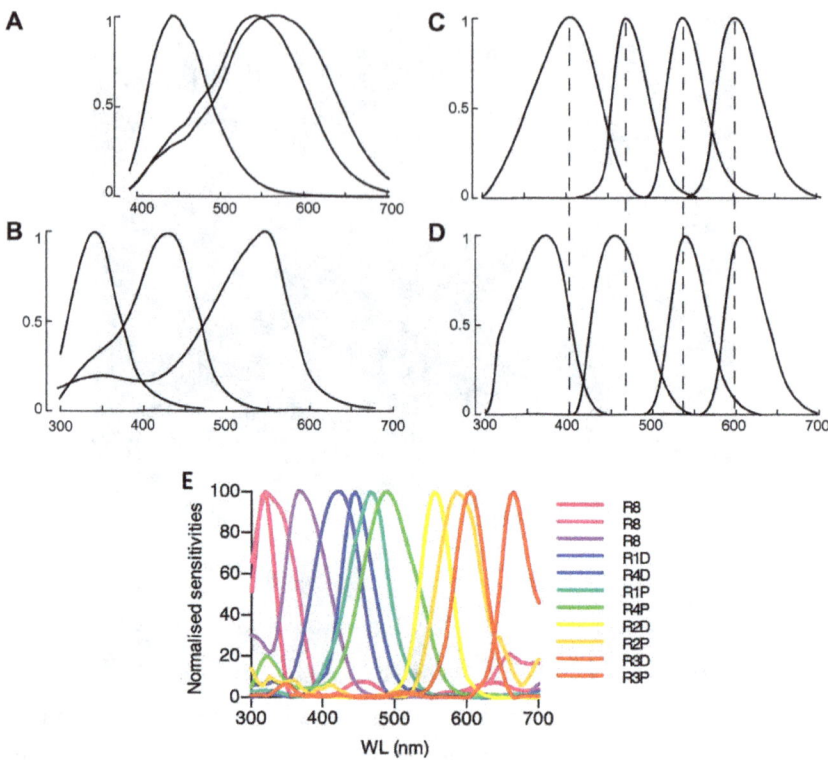

Figure 4 Photoreceptor variations. Normalized photoreceptor spectral sensitivities of: (a) human; (b) honeybee; (c) pigeon; (d) starling; (from Osorio and Vorobyev 2008, 2044) and (e) mantis shrimp (H. trispinosa) (from Thoen et al. 2014, 411).

instance, the flower's center reflects light in the ultraviolet range, as in Figure 5.

Notice that we have not yet discussed a problem, or at least not an argument. We have merely borne witness to some of what visual scientists have long known about perceptual variation; indeed, some of this is commonly known from ordinary experience. Perceptual variation might occur due to differences in background conditions, or lighting, or visual systems. Of course, much the same might be said for our experiences of temperature. If the air is cool, the water might feel warmer than it would have had the air been warm. If you are cold-natured, the water might feel cooler to you than to someone else. But although there is variation in how cool the water feels, there is a fact of the matter as to how warm the water is. Indeed, there is an objective fact of the matter as to how warm the water is; the water's temperature is independent of

Figure 5 Bee vision. The (a) image represents how a yellow flower will appear to normally sighted humans in normal lighting conditions, while the (b) and (c) images represent how the same flower may appear to bees (in the same lighting conditions). From https://steemitimages.com/DQmPbTh4se9BPgTEVSt6K7HLkHMKja9iWUChcNkR3vZj5Fk/Bee-Vision.jpg.

how it seems to us. So why think that perceptual variation challenges the view that objects are colored, or even that colors are objective features of objects, features that objects have independently of how they appear to us?

1.4 The Problems of Perceptual Variation

To begin, we should note that the problem of perceptual variation is at least two problems. The problems are often run together, and it is generally assumed that the two problems are essentially related. First, *the color problem*: given that different observers under different conditions view the colors of objects differently and given that we have no way to non-arbitrarily determine which observers and conditions to favor, how can there be a fact of the matter about an object's color? Second, *the color perception problem*: given that different observers under different conditions view the colors of objects differently and given that we have no way to non-arbitrarily determine which observers and conditions to favor, how can there be a fact of the matter as to which color experiences are veridical and which illusory?

It is easy to see why the two problems seem importantly related since you might think that an answer to either problem would provide an answer to the other. You might think, for instance, that if you knew the color of an object, then you would know which experiences are veridical. And you might think that if you knew which experiences were veridical, then you would know the colors of objects. Indeed, it is commonly thought that only by solving the second problem could the first be solved. How, after all, might we determine the colors of objects without first knowing which experiences are veridical? And if we have no way to determine the colors of objects, why believe that objects are colored? So, it is commonly thought that the problems are not only importantly related, but inseparable; and not only are the problems inseparable, but a solution for the first depends on a solution for the second.

And now we are ready to see how perceptual variation seems to threaten the view that objects are colored, especially once we accept that particular view of colors discussed in Section 1.2. According to that view, to know what color something is we must know exactly where in color space it belongs. Now take some object that appears unique blue (i.e., blue with no red or green in it) to me, but which appears blueish green to you. If my experience is veridical, then the object's color "fits" into that blue-space exactly between red and green. If your experience is veridical, then the object's color "fits" into that space between blue and green, but perhaps more toward blue. To determine where it fits, it is reasonable to think, we must determine which of us is seeing things aright. And now we seem faced with three options. Option 1: we are both seeing things aright, and so the object has two colors. Option 2: only one of us (or someone else) is seeing things aright, and so the other (or both of us) is experiencing a color illusion. Option 3: neither of us is seeing things aright, and neither is anyone else.

In Section 2 we will look at some recent influential accounts of colors and how each embraces one of the three options above. But it is worth pausing for just a moment to notice why each of the three options is, on the face of it, implausible.

Option 1 insists that objects are colored; colors are properties of objects, even if many of our intuitions about colors turn out to be false. Among the intuitions it seems forced to abandon is the intuition that nothing can simultaneously be two colors all over at the same time. After all, if I am seeing things aright, then the object is a pure blue. If you are seeing things aright, then the object is blueish green. If we are both seeing things aright, then the object has two different colors; it is simultaneously a pure blue and blueish green. Now it is worth pointing out that it is not a logical contradiction to claim that an object has two (or more) different colors all over at the same time. Although it is a contradiction to claim that the object is a pure blue and not, it is not a contradiction to claim that it is simultaneously a pure blue and another color. Still, there is a strong intuition that an object cannot have two different colors all over at the same time. That intuition, often called "the color incompatibility claim," is hard to give up. After all, it is one thing to say that something's color appears differently to different people, or at different times, or under different lighting; and yet another to say that something changes colors from time to time, like a chameleon; but something else entirely to say that it is, at a particular moment, uniformly many colors. That Jacob gave Joseph a coat of many colors is easy to imagine. That Jacob gave Joseph a coat that changes colors is easy to imagine, even if it is puzzling to understand how it might do that. That every coat has many different colors all over at the same time is neither easy to imagine nor to understand.[8]

Option 2 might seem to best fit our commonsensical understanding of colors and color perception. If you and I see an animal and I think we saw a dog, whereas you think we saw a bobcat, then surely at least one of us is mistaken. Nothing can be both a dog and a bobcat. And so, if it seems to me that the object is a pure blue, and it seems to you that it is blueish green, then surely one of us is mistaken. The problem, however, is that although we have a pretty good idea of what would make one of us right and the other wrong in the first case, we have no idea what makes one of us right and the other wrong in the second case. Given the variation in how we and other animals see colors, how do we decide on who the "right" observers are? And given the variation in how each of us sees colors relative to different backgrounds and lighting conditions, how do we decide on which viewing conditions are the "right" conditions? Since we have some independent idea of what it is to be a dog and what it is to be a bobcat, we know what would make one of us correct and the other incorrect in the first case, even if we will never know who was correct. But in the second case, if we have no way to specify who the right observers and conditions are, then how do we determine which objects are pure blue and which are not?

What motivates Option 3 are the problems for the other options. If nothing can simultaneously be two different colors all over at the same time, then Option 1 is untenable. And since we have no way to non-arbitrarily determine which observers and viewing conditions to favor, we have no non-arbitrary way to determine an object's color. Since we shouldn't be arbitrary, Option 2 is untenable as well. We then seem left with Option 3, that all color experiences are illusory. That was once the view of almost every philosopher from Descartes until the twentieth century.[9] Thomas Reid (1764) was one of the few holdouts. And it has been the view of many if not most scientists working on color perception since Galileo (1623). But it is worth remembering just how radical this view is, for it entails that every visual experience is at least partly illusory. When Aristotle claims that color is the proper object of sight, what he recognized was that all visual experience involves an experience of colors, and that no other sensory experience involves colors.[10] So, if every visual experience is a color-illusion, then every visual experience is at least partly illusory.[11]

---

[8] For a discussion of various color incompatibility claims, see Jody Graham (2002) and Frederik Gierlinger and Jonathan Westphal (2021).
[9] See Rene Descartes (1644/1988), John Locke (1690/1996), David Hume (1739).
[10] See Aristotle's *De Anima* (1941). Also see Kalderon (2015) for a recent discussion of Aristotle's views of color and perception.
[11] It is commonly assumed that visual perception necessarily involves color perception. Here we assume only that, as a matter of fact, human visual perception involves color perception. For

1.5 Coming Attractions

In the next section, after briefly discussing how we arrived at our current debates about colors, we canvas three different accounts (relationalism, objectivism, and eliminativism), each aligning with one of the three options discussed in Section 1.4. In Section 3, we present an alternative account of colors. Our suggestion is that a proper account of colors has escaped us because we got off on the wrong foot. A particular picture of colors held us captive and led us down the rabbit hole. We can, we will suggest, determine visually what color an object has without determining which color experiences are veridical. We can, in other words, solve the color problem without solving the color perception problem.

The account offered in Section 3 places a heavy emphasis on determinate colors, colors so determinate that we cannot easily reidentify them. In preparation for that, we explain in Section 1.6 how we are thinking about the determinate–determinable relationship. Section 3 then argues that we can determine the determinate colors of objects, so understood, without determining which color experiences are veridical. We first note that the popular view of colors that each color is essentially located in color space (see Section 1.2) is mistaken since, we argue, there are more colors, and even more colors that humans can visually discriminate, than there are locations in the color space commonly imagined; second, we argue that what makes a particular determinate color the particular color that it is isn't its location in color space. What makes a color distinct is that it makes a difference to color perception. Roughly, two objects are the same determinate color only if there are no observers who would see a color difference (e.g., a difference in hue, brightness, or saturation) between those objects under any lighting condition. For the most determinate of colors, David Hilbert (1987) is correct: if an observer sees a color difference between two objects and that difference is explained by (say) how those objects affect light, then it would be absurd to conclude that the observer's experience is illusory.

Section 4 has two aims. First, we directly confront the color perception problem, arguing that properly understanding that problem, regardless of how we solve it, supports the view that colors are objective properties of objects. We will be left, however, without an account of the more determinable colors that we commonly talk about. And so, second, Section 4 discusses the role of the more determinable colors. Section 4 makes room for the color determinables that we commonly talk about, colors determined by the more determinate colors discussed in Section 3. Many of those determinable properties are importantly anthropocentric. We care about those properties only, or at least primarily,

---

a discussion of why visual perception might not necessarily involve color perception, see Kathleen Akins and Martin Hahn (2015).

because we have the visual systems that we have, and this is reflected in the ways we commonly describe the colors of objects.

Here it will be important to separate two importantly different types of variation: perceptual variation and judgmental variation. How we think about perceptual variation with respect to the more determinable colors will depend partly on the theory of perception we accept, and here we attempt to remain neutral. Perhaps, for the more determinate of the determinable shades, only a select few observers represent objects as having the colors that those objects have.[12] Perhaps, instead, we should accept a pluralism about colors and conclude that perceptual variation entails that objects have as many colors as we and other animals see them as having.[13] Our point will be, regardless which way that goes, an objectivism about colors should be favored. Only objectivism can accommodate what seems true about the color incompatibility claim, and only objectivism can explain the perceptual agreement that we enjoy. (See Section 4.2.)

A pluralism about color judgments, however, must be restrained. Color language is a shared language, and its usefulness requires a certain amount of agreement. That agreement does not require exact agreement in how the colors of objects are perceived, but it does require general agreement about what it is appropriate to say. I must be able to ask someone to please bring the red folder from my desk and not, generally, be frustrated about which file they bring me.

In Section 5, we turn our attention to recent work in philosophy of science, biology, and mathematics that engages with objectivism, and we show how that work is relevant for thinking about colors. For instance, philosophers of mathematics often defend realism about mathematical entities by appeal to indispensability arguments. Very roughly, the idea is that we should be ontologically committed to what our best scientific theories cannot do without. Such arguments, we suggest, support an objectivism about colors when applied to examples from biology. We also propose an alternative way to think about color space, what we'll call "enhanced color space," such that our commonsense conceptions of colors are much like what we find in other domains of scientific inquiry. Finally, we will look at how realists about special science ontology employ concepts of scale-relativity, real patterns, realization, and emergence, and how such concepts might be employed in the context of colors. As we see there, the way in which we think of determinate colors and their determinables as being related in Section 4 is akin to the ways in which scientific realists think of higher-level kinds as related to more basic kinds.

---

[12] See, for instance, Byrne and Hilbert (2004).
[13] See, for instance, Yablo (1995), Watkins (2002), and Kalderon (2007).

Looking at recent work in biology and philosophy of science shows how our account of colors fits into a larger picture of the natural world.

1.6 Determinates and Determinables

Since much of what follows relies heavily on the determinate–determinable distinction, we need to discuss this distinction before going forward, especially since our use of the distinction is in some respects nonstandard. The history of the determinate–determinable relationship is beyond the scope of this Element.[14] This much, however, is generally assumed. Except for the most specific determinates and the most general determinables, what is a determinate of some determinable will also be a determinable of some other determinate; and what is a determinable of some determinate will also be a determinate of some further determinable. For instance, if an object is periwinkle, then its being periwinkle is a determinate of its being blue, and its being blue is a determinate of its being colored. The object's being blue, then, is both a *determinate* (of its being colored) and a *determinable* (of its being periwinkle). Put another way, the object's being periwinkle determines the way in which it is blue; and its being blue determines the way in which it is colored. Moreover, determination is transitive. If something's being periwinkle is a determinate of its being blue, and its being blue is a determinate of its being colored, then its being periwinkle is a determinate of its being colored. Our uses of "determinate" and "determinable" accord with these general assumptions.

It is sometimes assumed that if we know that some determinate is instantiated, then we thereby know which determinables are instantiated. If you know, for instance, that an object is periwinkle, then you must also know that it is blue. Here we part company with tradition. The relation we care about is a metaphysical relation, and not a conceptual relation. We follow Stephen Yablo (1992) who argues that, just as Saul Kripke (1980) taught us that some identities are knowable only a posteriori, some determinate–determinable relations are knowable only a posteriori as well. Yablo's suggestion is that some property P is a determinate of some property Q only if: necessarily, for all x, if x has P, then x has Q; and possibly, for some x, x has Q but lacks P. When John, say, visually discovers that two walls have the same determinate color, when John discovers that two walls match in color, that color shared by the walls is a determinate of the more determinable color or colors that the walls have. If the walls are blue, then anything having the determinate color of those walls will be blue. But for reasons that will become obvious later, we should not assume that

---

[14] For a discussion of that history, and much of the contemporary debate concerning it, see Jessica Wilson (2021a).

John is also aware of all the determinable colors shared by the walls simply in virtue of knowing the determinate color that it has.

It is also generally assumed that if a color is a determinate of some determinable at some level of specificity, then it cannot determine another determinable at the same level. If, for instance, some color is a determinate of being blue, then it cannot also be a determinate of being red. Here, we also part company with tradition. That very same determinate color that is yellow might also be another color for bees. Indeed, consistent with our view, an object might have more than one "human" color at the same determinable level.[15] The color incompatibility claim holds, we will insist, but only for the most determinate colors.

You might be tempted, at this point, to insist that what we are calling "determinate colors," although they might well explain colors, are not themselves colors. They are, after all, "shades of color" with no names. But this strikes us as highly implausible. If when comparing two objects against the same background and under some lighting condition, I see what I would naturally call "a difference in color," surely the right thing to say is that I see the objects as differently colored. Moreover, since that perceived difference is explained by the fact that those objects affect light differently, it would be odd to conclude that my experience is illusory. And since it is due to the objects' having those features that they have the more determinable colors that they have, it is natural to think of those features as determinate colors. Some object having some determinate color *determines* which determinable colors that object has. We will have much more to say about this in Sections 3 and 4.

2 A Brief History of the Problem and Possible Solutions

2.1 Some Background

Eliminativism about colors, the view that all color experiences are illusory, has ancient roots. Democritus, perhaps the first eliminativist, famously writes that "by convention sweet is sweet, bitter is bitter, hot is hot, cold is cold, color is color; but in truth there are only atoms and the void."[16]

Democritus' expressed motivation seems akin to Galileo's. Here is Galileo.

> Now I say that whenever I conceive any material or corporeal substance, I immediately feel the need to think of it as bounded, and as having this or that shape; as being large or small in relation to other things, and in some specific place at any given time; as being in motion or at rest; as touching or not touching some other body; and as being one in number, or few, or many. From these conditions I cannot separate such a substance by any stretch of my

---

[15] See Wilson (2013), Byrne and Hilbert (2006 and 2017), Watkins (2002), and Kalderon (2011).
[16] Ch. XVI, §II, 353 (Bakewell, Sourcebook in Ancient Philosophy, 1909, 60).

imagination. But that it must be white or red, bitter or sweet, noisy or silent, and of sweet or foul odor, my mind does not feel compelled to bring in as necessary accompaniments. Without the senses as our guides, reason or imagination unaided would probably never arrive at qualities like these. Hence I think that tastes, odors, colors, and so on are no more than mere names so far as the object in which we place them is concerned, and that they reside only in the consciousness. Hence if the living creature were removed, all these qualities would be wiped away and annihilated. But since we have imposed upon them special names, distinct from those of the other and real qualities mentioned previously, we wish to believe that they really exist as actually different from those (*The Assayer*, 23).

As stated, Galileo's argument is not compelling. Assuming that we can imagine a colorless world, it hardly follows that the world is colorless. From the mere fact that we would only believe something because it is reported by the senses is hardly reason to deny what our senses report. But what Galileo seems to have his sights on, and perhaps Democritus as well, is the thought that a completed scientific story of the universe will find no place for colors.

The color-problem, thought of this way, finds puzzling how we are to reconcile our ordinary conception of colors with what science tells us about the external world. This version of the color problem is what Wilfred Sellars (1962) describes as attempting to forge the scientific image with the manifest image, and the difficulty in accomplishing that task for colors is akin to the difficulty of accomplishing that task for ordinary objects and the ordinary properties that we commonly talk about. A completed physics will not mention automobiles or tables, we assume. It likely will not mention humans, either. Is there a special problem for colors? Many philosophers, most philosophers, have thought so.

Colors, unlike with shapes, can only be seen (just as tastes can only be tasted, and sounds can only be heard). Why would this alone motivate a skepticism about colors? The primary reason is that not only can we make sense of our being mistaken about shapes and sizes, but we have ways of determining which experiences and judgments concerning shapes and sizes are correct. For a feature to be objective, or at least for us to have any good reason to think that it is, we require some way to determine which experiences are veridical or which judgments are true. At least, that is the common thought. Since we have no way to determine the color of an object except by perception, there is no way to determine which color experiences are veridical except by appeal to other visual experiences. And since our visual experiences vary, and we have no reason to favor some observers over others, we seemingly have no way to determine what color something has. But if we have no way to determine what color something has, then we have no good reason to believe that anything is colored. This is the source of the problem of perceptual variation. Our focus for now is on the problem of perceptual variation.[17] We will have more to say about the role of colors in the scientific image of the world in Section 5.

So, say John and Susan disagree about the shape of an object. John sees it as square. Susan sees it as rectangular. Here we have a way, independent of John's and Susan's perceptions, to determine who is correct. We can measure the four sides to determine whether they are all the same length. We can measure the angles to determine whether they are all the same. Our measuring will also involve perception, of course, but presumably we can agree on what our measurements tell us. We have, in other words, a way of determining whether John or Susan is seeing or judging things aright. But now imagine that John sees a lemon as yellow, whereas Susan sees it as yellowish green. We might, of course, ask others to look, or have John and Susan look again and under different lighting conditions, but if none of these trials decides the matter, there seems to be no way to "measure," no way to determine whether it is John or Susan who is seeing the lemon aright. So, as tradition has it, shape is a primary property, an objective property of the object. Yellow is a secondary property, and a property that either doesn't exist in the object, or is at best relational, perhaps a property something has only in relation to an observer.[18]

We will mention, because it will matter for us later, that there are cases that seem to straddle the traditional demarcation. As we noted earlier, the water might feel cold to John, but merely tepid to Susan. That was, once upon a time, a reason to count heat as a secondary property. Of course, we have a way to measure temperature, even though this doesn't determine whether John or Susan is correct. Does water that is 65 degrees Fahrenheit count as cold or tepid? So, although we have a way to determine the temperature of water, it is not obvious that we have a way to determine which experiences are veridical. The temperature problem, determining the temperature of something, comes apart from the temperature experience problem, determining which experiences of temperature are veridical. In any case, it is not obvious that we have any way to "measure" colors. In addition, as we saw in Section 1, colors seem to have a complicated structure that makes perceptual variation especially perplexing. Susan sees the lemon as having some green in it, as we might say. John sees it as pure yellow. How could there be a fact of the matter about who is correct about that?

---

[17] For an excellent discussion of these two ways into the problem of colors, the reconciliation problem and the problem of perceptual variation, see Mazviita Chirimuuta (2015).

[18] See, for instance, Marshall and Weatherson (2018) for more on the intrinsic/extrinsic property distinction as well as how it compares to the relational/non-relational property distinction.

2.2 Eliminativism

For the eliminativist, the proponent of Option 3, the correct answer is that both John and Susan are mistaken. Nothing in the world answers to their color experiences. Perhaps the most influential contemporary argument for this position comes from Larry Hardin.[19] Hardin contends that, for a realist about color, there must be a fact of the matter about the color of the lemon. Since John and Susan perceive the color differently, at least one of them must be mistaken. But if there is a fact of the matter about an object's color, it must be possible to determine that fact visually, for otherwise it would seem that we are discerning facts about something other than the lemon's color. If an object appears darker against one background and lighter against another, which is it? How do we determine the "right" background? If an object appears to have one color under one lighting condition and a different color under a different lighting condition, which condition to favor? If an object appears unique blue to some but not to others, which observers to favor? If we cannot answer the earlier questions, then it seems we cannot meet Hardin's challenge. There seems not to be a fact of the matter about the colors of many objects that can be determined by looking at those objects.

Here is a way to appreciate the force of Hardin's argument, looking back at an example from Section 1. If we offer John a set of color chips ranging from chartreuse (greenish yellow) to orange (reddish yellow) and ask him to pick the chip that is pure yellow, and we ask Susan to perform the same task, they will likely choose different chips. They will disagree about where pure yellow lies. We might say that the color space for John is not the same as it is for Susan; perhaps better, their color spaces do not align. They have different "true yellows," like two compasses pointing "north" in different directions. But what could make it the case that either John or Susan is correct? We might appeal to some notion of "standard observer," and then claim that pure yellow is determined by what the standard observer chooses as pure yellow. But this move seems implausible. There is considerable variation in what seemingly normal human observers will choose as pure yellow. The *standard observer*, sometimes appealed to by scientists concerned with color vision, is simply an average, and different "standard observers" will be selected for different purposes. Put another way, whatever the standard observer would choose as pure yellow, no matter how that observer is chosen, most observers will see as slightly green or as slightly red. And, of course, the variety of color experiences expands considerably once we add nonhuman animals.

---

[19] See especially Hardin (1988 and 2003). Other notable eliminativists include Paul Boghossian and David Velleman (1989), David Chalmers (2006), Barry Maund (1995 and 2006), and Adam Pautz (2006).

But even if we could find reasons to favor some visual systems over all the others, that observer's experiences would vary considerably under different lighting conditions (see Figure 3), against different backgrounds (see Figure 2), and so forth. We might think that, since our visual experiences evolved for sunlight, sunlight counts as "normal." But sunlight, at least as that light illuminates objects on Earth, varies considerably. The light is more yellowish at midday, more blueish in the late afternoon. The light is filtered differently on cloudy days, and at different locations on the planet at different times of the year. It is true that an object's color will usually seem more or less the same across a range of lighting conditions, and especially across a range of daylight conditions, due to color constancy.[20] But differences in daylight conditions will sometimes result in significant changes in how an object appears, and even small changes would seem to make a response to Hardin's challenge seem daunting.

No doubt there are objective properties of the lemon, its reflecting certain light and absorbing other light, that partly explain why it looks as it does. And we have reason to believe that we can tell a complete scientific story about why any object appears as it does to any observer at any moment. But perceptual variation results from the fact that our visual systems are slightly different, and from the fact that our experiences vary under different lighting conditions and when objects are against different backgrounds. In other words, we can determine the lemon's reflectance properties, and the underlying physical properties that explain those, but on what grounds can we determine whether it is a pure yellow? If we cannot do that, Hardin argues, then we have no way to identify the lemon's color, and so no grounds for identifying its color (whatever it is) with any of its physical properties.

2.3 (Nonobjective) Relationalism

If we think an object's color cannot be *identified* independent of our experiences, then perhaps we should conclude that colors are not *identical* to properties independent of us. Perhaps we should conclude, instead, that something's color depends essentially on how that object is related to us.

A relation might, of course, be perfectly objective. "Kate is a/the daughter of Jody" expresses a relation between Kate and Jody. The relation is perfectly objective. Kate is (or is not) Jody's daughter regardless of what Kate or Jody believe or experience to be the case. And someone might think that colors are relational properties, but nonetheless objective. If you think, for instance, that

---

[20] See Keith Allen (2016, especially Chapter 2) for a recent defense of objectivism that relies on color constancy.

something has the color it has in virtue of how it interacts with light, then you seemingly think of colors as relational features of objects; but you nonetheless think that colors are objective features of objects.

One way to think about the objectivism/nonobjectivism distinction is by thinking about Plato's *Euthyphro*. Euthyphro thinks that to be righteous is to be loved by the gods; it is in virtue of the gods loving something that it is righteous. Socrates believes that, even if it were true that the gods love all and only what is righteous, the gods love what is righteous because it is righteous; the gods loving what is righteous does not make anything righteous. Euthyphro is a nonobjectivist about righteousness. Righteousness, for Euthyphro, might be independent of *our* judgments and experiences, but righteousness is not independent of judgment and experience. Socrates is an objectivist about righteousness. He believes that something's being righteous explains why the gods love it, for instance, and not the other way about.

"Relationalism," as we will use the term, refers to nonobjective relational accounts of colors. For the objectivist, something has the color it has independent of experience, and so colors explain color experiences, and not the other way about. For the relationalist, as we are using "relationalism," visual experiences at least partly explain what colors are.[21]

Dispositionalism, the view that an object's color is just its disposition to look a certain way to the right observers under the right conditions, is one such relational view. Dispositionalism was once commonly held in philosophy. Its popularity has waned.[22] One problem for such accounts is making sense of that certain way in which an object must appear to be a particular color. We cannot simply say that something is yellow just in case it would appear yellow. Such an account is obviously circular.[23]

An additional problem with such accounts, however, is that they seem unable to respond to Hardin's challenge. We might be tempted by the thought that for an object to be yellow is just for it to be such that it would appear yellow to the right observers under the right conditions. But as we have seen, it is unlikely that we can specify who those observers are and what those conditions might be with enough precision to counter Hardin's challenge.

---

[21] Some views do not fit well with our categorization. According to Alva Noë's (2004) "phenomenal objectivism", for instance, colors are patterns of relational appearances, but these patterns are objective features of the world. For us, this places Noë on the wrong side of the Euthyphro problem. Colors, on our view, partly explain those patterns of appearances. For more discussion, see Kalderon (Forthcoming) and Allen (2009).

[22] For a defense of dispositionalism see Colin McGinn (1983), Christopher Peacocke (1984), and Mark Johnston (1992).

[23] Indeed, the account would seem to be viciously circular. See Boghossian and Velleman (1989) and Watkins (1994).

Another relational strategy, developed by Jonathan Cohen (2009), argues that we should abandon all hope of specifying *the* color of an object. We should think of colors as relational properties of objects. That is, we should opt for Option 1 and allow that an object may have many different such relational properties.[24] If we treat colors as relational properties, and we treat objects, observers, and viewing conditions as the relevant relata, then every object might be thought of as having many colors. The lemon is yellow (in relation to John, the lighting conditions in which he currently sees the lemon, and against the lemon's current background) and it is yellowish green (in relation to Susan, and those same lighting conditions and background).

Cohen's thought is basically this. (1) John sees the lemon as yellow; Susan sees the lemon as yellowish green. (2) We have no reason to favor either John's experience or Susan's. (3) Since we have no reason to favor either, we should admit both; we should be "ecumenical." (4) The best way to be ecumenical is to think of colors as relational. Consequently, John and Susan each see *a* color of the lemon, but they don't see the same color of the lemon.

There is much to say about each step of this argument, both for and against.[25] As we will see in Section 4, we might be ecumenical and not think that colors are relational properties, at least as Cohen is thinking about it. Moreover, Cohen's strategy explicitly denies the color incompatibility claim, a motivation for Hardin's eliminativism. In any case, the options before us thus far treat every color experience either as illusory, concluding that nothing is colored, or as veridical, concluding that every object has very many colors.[26] So, if these are our only options, we seem forced either to conclude that nothing is colored or that the color incompatibility claim is false.

2.4 Objectivism

Perhaps we have made too much of the fact that we do not know how to choose between John and Susan, and so perhaps we were overly hasty in abandoning Option 2. After all, we can know that someone is mistaken without knowing who is mistaken. As we noted earlier, if John and Susan see an animal and John

---

[24] For other relational strategies see Thompson (1995) and Matthen (2005). Yet another strategy treats colors not as relations, per se, but as relative. On such accounts, nothing is yellow *simpliciter*. Instead, something is yellow relative to an observer under some condition. For a relativist, the lemon's having the property of being yellow (for John, under the conditions in which he sees the lemon) is that property of the lemon, whatever it is, that causes John's experience. But that very same property of the lemon that is yellow relative to John and the conditions in which he sees the lemon is yellowish green for Susan. See, for instance, Brogaard (2012) and McLaughlin (2021).

[25] See Watkins and Shech (2022) for a critical discussion of Cohen's argument.

[26] Cohen allows that there are some color illusions, but these are rare and irrelevant for what follows.

thinks he saw a bobcat, while Susan thinks that it was a dog, then surely at least one of them is mistaken. Of course, we may never know who was correct, or if they were both mistaken. But we are not tempted to conclude, simply because we will never know, that both were mistaken or that both were correct.

That said, the situation with colors seems importantly different. It is not just that, on occasion, we do not know who is correct. Rather, it seems that we never know and that there is no good reason to think that we ever will. Nonetheless, clearly there is a gap between our not knowing some fact, on the one hand, and there being no fact, on the other. Alex Byrne and David Hilbert (2004) aim to exploit this gap.[27]

Byrne and Hilbert think that colors are ways of affecting light. If, for simplicity, we think only of how the surfaces of objects reflect light, then we might think that colors are reflectance properties, or reflectance types.[28] If two objects reflect and absorb the same light, or if they reflect and absorb light in relevantly similar ways, then they have the same reflectance property or reflectance type; they are the same color. There are other ways to think about colors, consistent with objectivism. We might think that colors are those physical properties of objects responsible for their reflectance properties.[29] Alternatively, we might think that colors, although they are responsible for objects having the reflectance properties they have, are importantly sui generis; they are not reducible to other properties of objects.[30] For our purposes, these disagreements will not matter.

Hardin's challenge, remember, is that we must have a way to determine what color something is prior to our being able to identify a color with some physical property of the object. We can determine, for instance, the lemon's reflectance properties. But unless we know already whether the lemon is yellow or greenish yellow, we have no way to determine whether that reflectance property is yellow or greenish yellow. So, according to Hardin, we cannot solve *the color problem* without solving *the color perception problem*; if we have no reason to favor some color experiences over others, then we have no reason to think that there is a fact of the matter as to any object's color.

Byrne and Hilbert disagree. Even if we cannot determine which experiences are veridical, and even if we cannot determine exactly what color any object has, we have reason to believe that objects are colored. To both illustrate and motivate their response, Byrne and Hilbert tell a fanciful story. Imagine a kind of intelligent creature, Thermoms, who are endowed with a biological

---

[27] See Michael Tye (2006) for a similar position. For a reply to Tye, see Cohen, Hardin, and McLaughlin (2006). And for a reply to Cohen et al., see Byrne and Hilbert (2007).

[28] This is a simplification since light might also be dispersed, emitted, scattered, and so forth.

[29] See David Armstrong (1969) and J. J. C. Smart (1975).

[30] See Joshua Gert (2021 and 2008) and Watkins (2010).

thermometer that registers temperature. Thermoms generally agree about whether it is warm or cool, but their thermostats generally do not agree. While some Thermoms register 78 degrees, others will register 79, others 77, and so forth. Thermoms and their experiences of temperature are like us and our experiences of color, at least in some important respects. We generally agree about the colors of objects, at least for the more determinable colors. We generally agree about whether something is blue or red, for instance. Likewise, Thermoms generally agree about temperature. They generally agree about whether it is hot, or warm, or cold. Thermoms disagree, however, about exactly what the temperature is, just as we disagree about whether something is a pure blue.

The Thermoms, we might imagine, will never know what it is to be correctly calibrated. Perhaps there is a "right way" for Thermoms to be calibrated. Perhaps in Thermom's evolutionary history there was a favored way to be calibrated, and perhaps the best semantic theory of the Thermom language is such that "70 degrees" refers to whatever temperature was registered by that favored Thermom when it registered 70 degrees. Since there was little advantage to being precisely correct, however, variation occurred in the Thermom population, and those variations were passed on to Thermom children. But even though the Thermoms will never know who among them is calibrated in exactly the correct way, even though they will never know who among them is relevantly like their favored ancestors, there is no reason to think that there is not a correct way. Likewise, Byrne and Hilbert claim, for us and our color experiences.

Not surprisingly, many philosophers have not been convinced. Byrne and Hilbert are certainly correct that it doesn't follow from our not knowing the right way to be calibrated, either for Thermoms or for us, that there is not a right way to be calibrated. But even if we grant that there might be a right way, we seem to have little reason to believe that there is.

It is interesting, however, that even if we can never know which Thermom is correct, we are not tempted either by an eliminativism or a relationalism about temperature. Thermoms experience temperature, and we have every reason to think that there is an objective property in the world that they are experiencing. Why not think the same about colors? One reason seems to be this: although we expect that there is an objective property associated with temperature – we can measure it, after all – we don't expect, or at least many don't expect, an objective property to be associated with colors. We return to this worry in Section 4.1.

As will become obvious in the next section, our sympathies are with Byrne and Hilbert. We agree with Byrne and Hilbert that *the color problem* can be solved without solving *the color perception problem*. However, we think that Byrne and Hilbert, along with most everyone in the color debate, have made a fundamental mistake about what is required to visually determine the color of an object, the mistake that led us all down the rabbit hole.[31]

3 Out of the Rabbit Hole

3.1 Learning about Colors

Various intuitions about color perception inform many philosophical discussions about colors. It is sometimes thought, for instance, that colors are manifest properties; vision provides immediate access to colors.[32] We might think, even, that visual experience is revelatory; that color experience reveals to us the underlying nature of colors.[33] Minimally, it might be thought, color experience is epistemically privileged.[34] If Susan is a normal observer and under normal lighting conditions, and something appears green to Susan, then it must be green.

Whatever might be said about those intuitions, we need to keep in mind some of the more commonplace ways that we think and talk about colors. For instance, we often take ourselves to learn more about an object's particular color across lighting conditions, while comparing an object's color to the colors of other objects, and so forth. At the very least, we commonly take ourselves to gain more information about how an object's particular color looks under various conditions, the way the object's color appears under various lighting conditions and when placed against variously colored objects.

How best to think about *looks* is a complicated issue.[35] Here we are thinking of a color's various *looks* not as its appearing to be different colors. When John recognizes that the color of his tie clashes with the color of his shirt, John does not thereby see the color of his tie as a different color than he did before; nor does he see the color of his shirt as a different color than he did before. When Susan holds a paint sample up to her wall and realizes that the paint sample is a bit more reddish than her wall, she does not thereby see the color of the sample as differently colored than she did before; nor does she see the color of her wall as differently colored than she did before. But Susan and John do see something about the colors of those objects that they had not seen before. Susan sees that her paint sample is more reddish than her wall; John sees that the color of his tie classes with the color of his shirt.

That we acquire more information about an object's color under different viewing conditions becomes more obvious as we reflect on how people who

---
[31] Mark Eli Kalderon (2007) is a notable exception.   [32] See Mark Johnston (1997).
[33] See Johnston (1992).   [34] See Allen (2016).
[35] Those most influential for us are M. G. F. Martin (2006), Charles Travis (2013), Kalderon (2007 and 2011), J. L. Austin (1962), Myles Burnyeat (1979), and Sydney Shoemaker (2003 and 2006).

work with colors, work with colors. Interior decorators work with various paint samples, looking carefully at each in the context of the room with its furniture, paintings, and lighting, and then paint large areas of a room to see how it looks at different times of the day and under different natural and artificial lighting. For an artist, spending much of her time thinking about the palette of colors before her, the entire artistic enterprise involves learning more about colors. An artist continually makes "color adjustments as she works. Each introduction of a new color requires a reworking of the existing colors."[36]

Much of the visual information that we commonly take ourselves to gather about an object's color comes when we compare its color to the color of other objects, and when we look at an object's color across various lighting conditions. It is by putting objects side by side that we determine how various colors look together. We also often find out whether two objects match in color. Susan may simply look at her wall to see that it is blue, and she need only look at various paint samples at the store to see whether they are blue or not, but she would never simply go to the store and attempt to match a paint with the color that she remembers her wall to be. It is hard enough to match socks.

Determining whether the colors of two objects match, or whether they are different, raises the question of what our *standards* are for two objects to be the same color. That question, as asked, is certainly ambiguous. As Aristotle reminded us long ago, "precision is not to be sought for alike in all discussions."[37] Artists, interior decorators, and automobile body repair-folk employ similar standards for sameness of color, and that is the standard most of us use most of the time. Two objects match in color if, when viewed pairwise against the same background, we (common folk) cannot see a color difference under the various lighting conditions under which we commonly see those objects. And so, according to this standard, if two objects appear differently in color when viewed pairwise by a normal human observer against the same background and under the same lighting, then those objects have different determinate colors; they do not match.

Of course, that ordinary standard may not be precise enough for certain purposes, and especially for certain scientific purposes. For a scientist comparing the color vision of various animals, for instance, our ordinary standard will prove insufficient.[38] Bees, recall, are sensitive to light in the ultraviolet range, but not in the red range. Consequently, if two objects reflect the same light within the range to which we are sensitive and only one of the objects reflects light in the ultraviolet range, the objects will appear the same in color to us but not to bees. For instance, as illustrated in Figure 5, some flowers that appear

---

[36] From filmmaker Hollie Lavenstein (personal correspondence).
[37] Aristotle (1941), 936 (*Nicomachean Ethics*, Bk 1, Ch. 2, 194b, lines 13–14).
[38] See, for instance, Gerald Jacobs (1981).

uniformly colored to us will have a different color toward their center that is visible to bees (serving as a target for their nectar gathering activity). So, is the flower uniformly yellow, or is the center a different color to which we are blind? Each answer is plausibly correct, depending on the standards we employ. A far stricter standard than the one we humans commonly employ, but one more appropriate to a scientist studying comparative vision, might hold that if two objects appear differently in color to any animal when viewed pairwise against the same background and under the same lighting, across the range of all lighting conditions, then those objects have different determinate colors; they do not match, relative to that standard.

The discussion above presupposes that objects are colored, but that is more than we wish or need to assume. Understand those assumptions as conditional on colors being instantiated. If objects are colored, here is how you can determine that two objects have the same or different colors, relative to certain standards; here is how colors can be differentiated. If objects are colored, here is how you can gain more information about an object's color. If there are no colors, then our apparent discriminations and information gatherings are either illusory or concern features other than colors. We are making assumptions about how particular colors are individuated and how information about those colors is acquired, assumptions supported by our everyday practices. These assumptions, of course, run counter to eliminativism and relationalism, and so might seem question-begging. But those views are motivated largely by worries about perceptual variation, and that is our target here. In any case, our primary aim is not to support a particular theory about colors, although it is *an* aim to narrow the viable options. Primarily, we aim to show that we – philosophers and others working on color – have made it seem harder than it is to determine the colors of objects. Indeed, we have made it seem nearly impossible. That has made arguments from perceptual variation seem far more powerful than they are, and it has made an objectivism about colors seem far less plausible than it is.

3.2 Revisiting Perceptual Variation

In Section 1 we looked at some of the ways in which color experiences vary. A gray color square against a light background will have a darker look than the same square against a darker background, as illustrated in Figure 2. Objects that seemingly match in color under certain lighting conditions and to some observers might look radically different in color under another lighting condition, and even to those same observers, as illustrated in Figure 3. Those objects that look unique blue to John (that appear to be blue with no red or green in them) might appear quite reddish or greenish to Susan, even against the same backgrounds and under the same lighting conditions.

This is only data about how colors appear, and in Section 2.2 we looked at why this data might suggest that there are no colors. Let's look at the argument again, but in greater detail. One way to think about how such an argument goes is by appealing to certain "principles" seemingly essential to colors, but incompatible with what we now know about perceptual variation. Hardin begins by telling us:

> [There are] two principles to which the color realist ought to subscribe. The first principle is that an object's having a given color is a matter of fact. To adhere to this principle is to be a realist about color. According to the second principle, it is normally possible to determine what color a thing has by looking at it (2003, 191).

Hardin believes, along with many others, that these principles conflict with well-known empirical facts about color experience. If an object appears darker against one background and lighter against another, which is it? How do we determine the "right" background? If an object appears to have one color under one lighting condition and a different color under a different lighting condition, which condition to favor? If an object appears unique blue to some but not to others, which observers to favor? If we cannot answer the earlier questions, it might seem that Hardin's two principles are violated. There seems not to be a fact of the matter about the colors of objects that can be determined by looking at those objects.

Hardin's two principles seem reasonable, and they seem to conflict with much that we now know about color and color experience. But a closer look at Hardin's principles shows either that those principles are not reasonable, or that no conflict arises. Let's take them in order.

The first. To be a realist about color, Hardin tells us, is to hold that an object's having a given color is a matter of fact. Compare: to be a realist about length is to hold that an object's length is a matter of fact; to be a realist about size is to hold that an object's size is a matter of fact; to be a realist about temperature is to hold that an object's temperature is a matter of fact. These claims certainly seem plausible, but it is easy to lose your confidence once you move from an object's determinate length or size to its more determinable length and size. An object has whatever determinate length it has. It might be the length of another, for instance. It might be exactly 6 meters long, at least relative to some standard of precision. An object has the determinate size it has. It might weigh what another weighs; it might be as tall as another; it might weigh twenty stones and be fourteen hands tall, for instance. But is it long or large? Is it heavy or light?

Of course, "long," "large," and so forth are relative predicates. Something might be a large animal, but a small elephant. But even fixing the relation will not always make obvious whether the predicate applies or not. Now this is arguably all due to vagueness, and not every disagreement about colors seems to be merely a matter of vagueness. Perceptual differences of colors can be stark, even if they usually are not. But our point here is only that Hardin's first principle is far more obvious for determinate colors than for determinable colors. The realist about length must hold that there is a fact of the matter about what length something has; she need not hold that there is always a fact of the matter about whether something is long. The realist about temperature must hold that there is a fact of the matter about something's temperature; she need not hold that there is always a fact of the matter about whether something is warm as opposed to merely tepid. So, to read the first principle in a way that makes it obviously true for the realist, we should understand Hardin this way: an object's having a given determinate color is a matter of fact.

Hardin's second principle is that "it is normally possible to determine what color a thing has by looking at it." The thought that colors are intimately tied to visual experience has ancient roots. But on a natural reading of Hardin's second principle, realism seems unthreatened. We often agree about whether something is blue, for instance, simply by looking at it.[39] Likewise, we can often tell whether something is large or long by looking at it. Of course, there are cases where, arguably, we cannot tell whether something is blue. Perhaps it is a borderline case, or perhaps its appearance changes radically under different seemingly normal lighting conditions. Similarly, sometimes we cannot determine whether something is long or large simply by looking at it, either because it is a borderline case, or because the angle makes it difficult to decide, or because it is in a medium like water that alters the look of its size and shape. But none of this seems especially threatening to an objectivism about colors.

What Hardin needs is a principle that is both plausibly true of what colors *must* be, but one that seemingly cannot be met given the empirical data. Perhaps: it is normally possible to determine what *determinate* color a thing has by looking at it. Now we should not assume, as we might for the more determinable colors, that we can normally determine on any single occasion something's determinate color by looking at it. That principle would run contrary to other very plausible assumptions discussed in Section 3.1. If, under different visual circumstances, we learn more about an object's

---

[39] To be clear, we aren't claiming that there is general agreement about the set of all blue objects, or whether any particular object is uniquely blue. Our claim is that, for most objects, there is agreement about whether that object is blue. Were this not so color language would be of little use.

determinate color, then we cannot assume that, on any visual occasion, we can determine an object's determinate color by sight. That is not to say that we cannot *see* an object's determinate color on any occasion; it is only to say that our seeing an object's determinate color on any occasion will not generally allow us to know its determinate color, to know whether it will match the colors of certain other objects across observers and lighting conditions. Compare: I can see a stick that is 6.25 inches long, but I cannot know from that experience that it is 6.25 inches long (as opposed to 6.22 inches long) without measuring it. Nonetheless, the assumptions with which we started are certainly compatible with our being able to determine an object's determinate color by sight, at least relative to our ordinary standards. Those assumptions suggest only that determining an object's determinate color by sight may take considerable visual work, looking at the object under different lighting and against different backgrounds, comparing how the object looks alongside other objects, and so forth.

In responding to Hardin, Byrne and Hilbert (2004) understand Hardin's second principle as concerning determinate shades, as we suggest earlier, but they nonetheless deny Hardin's second principle:

> Although there is much agreement on what is green, dark-green, and yellowish green, there is not much agreement on what possesses the highly determinate shades, like unique green. According to reflectance physicalism (and many other theories of color), some objects are unique green, and yet, with a fixed choice of viewing conditions, such objects will appear unique green only to a minority of normal perceivers. If, as Hardin says, 'No scientific sense can be attached to the claim that some of the observers are perceiving the color of the stimulus correctly and others not', then reflectance physicalism is false (41–42).

So, Byrne and Hilbert take the issue to be whether there is a fact of the matter about the determinate colors of objects, and they take the unique shades to count as examples of determinate shades. But Hardin's second principle is dropped. We are no longer requiring that we can tell, by looking at the object, what its determinate color is. We now require only that we can make scientific sense of the claim that some observers are correct, while others are not. And, indeed, Byrne and Hilbert grant, at least for the sake of argument, that we cannot tell by looking at an object what its determinate color is. They grant, then, that Hardin's second principle cannot be met. Indeed, they grant, for the sake of argument, that it might never be met:

> Let us ... concede, again for the sake of the argument, that this deficiency in our knowledge [that is, our inability to determine exactly which determinate color an object has] is an irremediable part of the human condition. In particular, the theory of perceptual representation will never advance to the

point where we will have some 'independent method,' as Hardin says (199), for determining exactly which properties our color experiences represent objects as having. Now unless we make some controversial verificationist assumption, it is hard to see why this scenario makes "no scientific sense," or is otherwise objectionable (2004, 42).

Now, in general, it is a mistake to assume that what something is and whether we can know what it is go hand in hand. That kind of mistake is the mistake that Byrne and Hilbert caution us against. We ordinarily determine whether something is water by how it looks and tastes, and nothing about how we typically determine whether some liquid is water informs us that water is essentially composed of H_2O. We might never have known that water is H_2O even though it nonetheless is. But it must be said, in Hardin's defense, that an object's color and its appearance seem intimately related. That there are colors that we cannot see (but bees can, e.g.,) is not a problem for objectivism, or at least not the problem that we face here. It is well known that objects can affect light in very many ways, and that animals are sensitive to light in different ways. We should expect, then, that different animals see different colors. Consequently, objectivists commonly adopt a pluralism about colors, at least for the more determinable color categories.[40] As we have seen, the flower that appears uniformly yellow to us, might appear to a bee to have two distinct colors. The bee, being sensitive to ultraviolet light, sees a difference to which we are blind. It is plausible, too, that we see a sameness that the bee does not. The flower uniformly reflects light in the non-ultraviolet range, a feature to which the bee is perhaps blind.

It is important to keep in mind that the challenge for color realism arises not from perceptual variation alone. One subject sees the object as a pure blue, the other as a greenish blue. If we cannot determine which subject's experience is veridical, the reasoning goes, how can we determine visually what color something has? And to concede that we can never tell by sight what color something has, and even that we cannot tell by any known means what colors we are seeing, is to concede much. Whether it is to concede so much that objectivism must fail is open to debate, and that is a debate that we will not attempt to resolve. For Byrne and Hilbert, there are two questions, and they are separable. First, can we determine the determinate color of an object visually? Second, can any scientific sense be made of there being a fact of the matter about an object's determinate color? Hardin takes these questions to be inseparable. He believes that whatever physical property we identify with a color must align with what can be discriminated visually, for otherwise we have no reason to think that what we are identifying with a physical property is a color. That is what motivates his

---

[40] See, for instance, Watkins (2002) and Kalderon (2007).

insistence that whatever colors are, they must be such that we can determine which color something has by sight alone. Since the determinate colors cannot be determined visually, according to Hardin, objectivism fails. Byrne and Hilbert grant that we cannot determine the determinate colors of objects visually, but they argue that we can nonetheless make "scientific sense" of objects having determinate colors.

What both parties accept is that we cannot, perhaps ever, visually determine an object's determinate color. We will now suggest that both parties are mistaken. We can perfectly well make sense of determining an object's determinate color visually once we are clear about what the task requires. Once we have done that, we can satisfy Hardin's second principle, properly understood, and perfectly well make sense of the claim that colors are (identical to or realized by) physical properties. Just what those physical properties are and how best to think about them are further questions, and questions we leave for another day.

To recap, we argued that Hardin's first principle is plausible for the most determinate colors, but it is consistent with objectivism to reject the first principle for determinable colors. Hardin's second principle is plausible for determinable colors (and commonly satisfied), but it is not plausible for the most determinate colors on any single viewing occasion and without specifying standards. We now show how we can satisfy Hardin's two principles, properly understood.

3.3 Determining Determinate Colors

What is required of us to visually determine the determinate color of an object?[41] What, exactly, must we be able to do? It is certainly not required that we be able to name the color, for we may not yet have a word for it. For very determinate shades we do not, and that is at least partly explained by our inability to remember very fine-grained shades of color. Furthermore, as we noted earlier, it is not required that we be able to visually determine an object's determinate color on any occasion. Determining visually that two objects have different determinate colors might require a considerable amount of work. We might have to look at the objects under a wide range of lighting conditions, for instance. Consequently, visually determining, at least with much confidence, that two objects have (at least very nearly) the same determinate color will often require considerable work, and this is especially so if our standards are very exact.

---

[41] We would be remiss not to note our debt to Hilbert (1987) and Kalderon (2007) who convinced us that the metaphysical status of colors depends more on the status of determinates than on determinables. Also see Churchland (2007). In what follows, we hope to provide further motivation for their insight.

Perhaps what is being required is that we be able to locate an object's color on a color chart or find its exact location on a color wheel. Indeed, we suppose that something like this is what Hardin, along with Byrne and Hilbert, assume to be both necessary and sufficient for determining an object's determinate color. This is the view of colors that we discussed in Section 1. That would explain why the unique shades play a pivotal role in many debates about the objectivity of colors. To be unique blue is to have that color that is located at that very particular location in color space; in the blue-space but leaning neither toward red nor toward green. If a color essentially has a particular hue, saturation, and brightness, then it presumably will have a particular location. Hardin would then be insisting that we must be capable of visually determining where an object's color is located in color space if colors are objective properties of objects; since we cannot, objectivism fails. Byrne and Hilbert concede that we cannot determine this visually, or at least we cannot know which observers can and which cannot, but that this does not prevent us from making "scientific sense" of an object's color having a particular location in color space, even if we can never know exactly where in color space it belongs. As we will now show, both parties to this dispute are requiring too much.

What we mean by "color space" is, again, what we take to be commonly represented by three-dimensional representations of the various color experiences that we might have, such as in Figure 1. In Section 1, we offered this way of thinking about how a representation of color space is created. We know, of course, that two objects that are slightly different in color – that two objects that are slightly different in hue, saturation, or brightness – might appear the same even for the most acute human observer. O_1 and O_2 might be indiscernible in color when viewed pairwise, and O_2 and O_3 might be indiscernible in color when viewed pairwise, yet O_1 and O_3 might be discernible in color when viewed pairwise. Consequently, you might fail to recognize a genuine difference in color while carefully comparing the colors of two objects.

Of course, you no doubt recognize a similarity as well, perhaps even a sameness. If O_1 is periwinkle, then quite plausibly O_2 is periwinkle as well. The objects are not only alike in being blue, but they are also alike in being that shade of blue, periwinkle blue. But whatever we ultimately want to say about *this* notion of "being the same shade of color," the relation is not transitive. So even if we conclude that O_1 and O_2 are the same shade of blue (since they appear the same shade of blue, periwinkle, to normal observers under normal conditions), periwinkle is obviously *a determinable relative to some further determinate*. O_1 and O_2 might be the same shade of blue, but *they are not the same ultimately determinate color.* They must not be since we can visually determine their difference when we compare them to O_3. Or, to put the matter another way, there are reasonable standards for the sameness of color, reasonable at least for certain purposes, according to which O_1 and O_2 are not the same color.

To determine visually whether two objects have (at least more precisely) the same color, we need to compare them with the colors of other objects. Two objects are the same determinate color, then, only if they match all *and only* the same objects with respect to color. In the case above, you can discriminate O_1 and O_2 visually, but only by comparing each to O_3. Each point in color space, then, can be discriminated from any other, but not always by pairwise comparisons alone. We might think, then, that we have a representation of color space that is saturated. No space is left unoccupied, at least so long as we are thinking that there is a color for and only for every possible color experience any normal human observer might have.

Now let's return to our discussion of Hardin, and Byrne and Hilbert, and ask two questions. First, can we determine visually where in color space an object's color lies? Second, is being able to do so requisite for objectivism?

The first question is ambiguous, and that ambiguity plays a central role in what follows. We might ask two subjects to match an object's color to a color on a chart, for instance. Or we might ask two subjects to determine on a chart where unique blue is located. The subjects might well agree while performing the former task even if they fail to agree on the latter. Indeed, subjects will generally agree about whether two objects have the same color even though they disagree about which shades are unique blue or unique green. Compare: most humans can at least be trained to recognize whether two musical notes are the same; most humans cannot determine by sound whether the note they heard was a C_4. We can now consider two possible tasks, each of which we might understand as a requirement for objectivism.

Matching: can we determine visually whether some object matches in color some color in color space or on some color chart? Can we determine whether two objects have the same color or different colors?

Locating: can we determine visually whether some location in color space or on some color chart is unique blue?[42]

To understand what we have in mind, consider the Xs below (in Figure 6). Most observers will initially see the X on the left as gray and the one on the right as yellow. Asking whether the Xs are yellow or gray is a "locating" question. Answering whether the Xs are the same color is a "matching" question. If you look at where the

---
[42] Our way of putting this distinction was influenced by Kate Graham, in conversation.

Figure 6 Matching Xs. The Xs are qualitatively identical, but there is an obvious difference in their color appearance. From Greenfieldboyce (2014).

Xs meet at the bottom, you see that the answer to the matching question is "yes," and that question we can answer even though we have not determined what color the Xs are; we have not yet answered the "locating" question.

Just how challenging our first task (*Matching*) is depends, as we noted earlier, on the standards that we employ. If our standards are very strict, if we require that objects match in color across all lighting conditions and all perceivers, including other types of animals, then we cannot find the color of every object we might wish to match in the kind of color space represented by Figure 1 since, by that standard, there are more colors than there are points in that representation of color space. Indeed, if our standard is strict enough, then we might wonder whether any two objects are the same color, at least if they do not have exactly the same reflectance profiles. The same might be said of length or temperature, of course. That is why, to channel Aristotle, such strict standards are rarely useful.

As we saw earlier, two objects match metamerically if and only if they appear the same in color for an observer under some lighting condition, even though they have different reflectance profiles. It is, for instance, physically possible for an object painted partly with one paint and partly with another to appear uniformly colored to normal human perceivers under some lighting condition even though the two paints reflect none of the same light.[43] Of course, the object will not appear uniformly colored under all lighting conditions and to all normal human perceivers. The reason is that, since the two paints reflect radically different proportions of light from different spectral ranges, we can place the object under a lighting condition in which those different spectral reflectance properties will be visually obvious.

---

[43] See Edward Averill (1985) for a discussion of such a case.

Now imagine three objects: O_4, O_5, and O_6. O_4 appears blue under all daylight conditions. O_6 appears purple under all daylight conditions. O_5 is a metameric match for both O_4 and O_6, but under different daylight conditions,[44] and O_5 is always a match for one or the other[45] (see Figure 3). O_5 might be the same shade of blue as O_4 and not the same shade of purple as O_6, or vice versa. Alternatively, we might conclude that O_5 is both that particular shade of blue and that particular shade of purple, or that it is not the same as either. Our point is that, however O_5 is classified more determinably, it is obviously not the same determinate shade of color as either O_4 or O_6, at least relative to certain standards. The reason is simple, and it is for much the same reason that we might treat O_1 and O_2 as differently colored. We can discriminate a color difference between O_5 and O_4 under some viewing conditions, and we can discriminate a color difference between O_5 and O_6 under some viewing conditions. We can see a color difference, and surely our experience of that difference is not illusory. But, notice, there is no location in the color space we have imagined to locate O_5's color unless we place it with the color of O_4 or O_6, despite its not having the same determinate color as either. Thus, there are more determinate colors that we can see, and that we can visually discriminate, than there are points in color space; or, perhaps more intelligibly, color space is far more complex than the representations of color space with which we are most familiar. (See Section 5.3 for how we might think about a more complex representation of color space.)

For the sake of discussion, let us take this to be our standard for sameness of color: Two objects match in color if and only if no human observer under any lighting condition in which humans view objects, while viewing the objects side by side and against the same background, can see a color difference between those objects.[46] Again, this is not the only acceptable standard. If we wish to know how to discern all of the colors visible to any creature, the standard employed here will be insufficient. But can we – consistent with this standard, a standard for discriminating the colors that humans see – determine whether two objects match in color? Sure. We do it all the time. We generally agree about whether two objects match in color, at least when given the opportunity to look

---

[44] Talk of "standard daylight conditions" hides the fact that the sunlight reaching Earth's surface is filtered differently at different times of the day, at different seasons of the year, and at different locations on the globe.

[45] This is for simplicity. What needs to be the case, and presumably would be, is that O_5 will always be a metameric match for some color purportedly having some location in color space.

[46] Notice that our standard favors no particular observer or lighting condition. What makes it the case that two objects match in color, relative to a standard, is that they cannot be discriminated in color by any observer in any lighting condition relevant to that standard.

at those objects side by side across various viewing conditions.[47] And not only do we agree, but we have every reason to believe that there is a perfectly good scientific explanation for what it is that we are agreeing about.

It is worth noting that our account allows that there are no abnormal observers, at least relative to certain standards. If an "abnormal" observer sees a color difference that we do not, then there is a difference to which we are blind. Of course, that observer may fail to see a similarity that we do, and that failure may result in her making color judgments that are false. We will return to this possibility in Section 4.5. Here we note only that, on our account, such an observer achieves a visual success, even if her success leads to an error in judgment.

3.4 Taking Stock

What we have argued for here will seem, from a certain perspective, radical. It seems to many a necessary truth that each color has a particular hue, saturation, and brightness; that each color essentially occupies a particular location in color space. Given that assumption, and given the popularity of representational accounts of perception, it is natural to think, too, that color perception represents an object's color as belonging to some location in color space. If something appears more greenish to me than to you, then we are representing the object as having different colors, as having different locations in color space. And so, either colors are highly relational, or colors are never instantiated. If there is no fact of the matter about which experiences are veridical and which not, then there is no fact of the matter about that object's color.

We have argued that colors are not essentially located in color space (Section 3.3), or at least not in the kind of color space represented by Figure 1, and we are agnostic about whether there is a "right" way for a color to be experienced (see Section 4.1). It is certainly essential to colors that they are the features that we see. And even though what colors are and how we know about them are separable, our epistemology and our metaphysics must be compossible. Furthermore, as Hardin rightly insists, if anything is colored, then surely one way to know that is by looking at it.

But thinking that there is a uniquely "right" way for a color to appear ignores the very many ways that a color appears. When we ask what someone sees when they see a particular color, when we ask what knowledge was acquired from their experience, their answers will generally appeal to our shared color

---

[47] Of course, some objects might be too small to match (they would look the same as some other object were they larger) or it might be judged differently because of its shape (and so would have to be placed on top of another object) or it might vary in appearance depending on which angle the light strikes it or the angle from which it is perceived (see Section 3.4).

concepts. "It looks red," someone might answer. Now we certainly do not wish to deny that some objects are red, no more than we wish to deny that boiling water is hot. Something that is red will surely look red, at least to most of us most of the time. But the very particular color that something has, the very particular color that we see, is complex, as is the phenomenology of color experience.

Here is an example to help illustrate our point, and one that might well seem opposed to the objectivism that we endorse. The exterior walls of the laboratory wing of the SUNY Upstate Medical Institute for Human Performance are all of the same siding panels.[48] But, as we might describe it, the colors of the panels look very different, and this is all due to the angle from which each panel is viewed. What color are the panels? Surely there must be an answer to this question if their color is objective, Hardin will insist. But what is being insisted upon is once again that we be able to *locate* the color of the panels. We assume that if a panel is destroyed, that it will be replaced by one of the same color; one that *matches* the other panels (see Section 3.3).

Patrick O'Brian offers up this beautiful description: "it was one of those days when some particular quality in the light and not merely the brilliance of the sun makes colours glow and sing . . .." (77). If two objects have the same color, they must glow and sing alike. And some colors glow and sing in such a way that they are impossible to locate in color space, at least as we commonly think of color space. Indeed, there may be no way to categorize the color of some objects, at least given the determinable color categories that we commonly employ. None of this, we have argued, is reason to deny that they have exactly the colors that they have.

4 Reweaving the Rainbow

4.1 Which Experiences Are Veridical?

We argued in Section 3 that we can visually determine the determinate colors of objects, at least in the sense of being able to determine whether two objects are colored the same or differently relative to a standard of sameness. But even if we can, over a range of lighting conditions, distinguish between different determinate colors, can we determine which of our experiences is veridical on any occasion on which our experiences vary? Perhaps John sees an object as unique green (he detects no blue or yellow in it), whereas Susan sees the object as greenish blue. John and Susan agree on which objects have the same determinate color, at least when given the opportunity to view objects over a range of

---

[48] Our thanks to Larry Hardin for this example (personal correspondence).

conditions. But is it John or Susan who is seeing things aright on this occasion? Hardin, once again, from an earlier work (1988):

> We are perhaps initially inclined to say that at least one of them must be wrong as a matter of natural fact. But, since we have no independent physical criteria for the identity of hues, we are obliged to fall back on some form of stipulation (89).

Now there are two arguments suggested by this passage, and they are easily run together. If the argument assumes that, since our experiences of any object's color might differ, we have no way to determine an object's determinate color, then we have already provided reasons to reject that assumption. We can, after all, determine whether two objects have the same or different colors relative to whichever reasonable standard we care about. But perhaps the argument is, instead, that objectivism requires that we be able to determine which experience is veridical where our experiences differ. Since we cannot do that, objectivism fails. That these issues are importantly different becomes obvious once we realize that the second argument relies, at least implicitly, on a certain way of thinking about perception, in general, and on a way of thinking about color perception, in particular. Most importantly, the argument assumes that a representational theory of perception is correct. Otherwise, we can make no sense of experiences misrepresenting. If we think of perception presentationally, if we think that perception immediately presents the world to us, then experiential differences might be explained by other differences in what we see and differences in how we see what we see. We might think, for instance, that we see not only a colored object, but a colored object lit in a particular way, from a certain angle, while shaded or not; perhaps, even, we see different determinable colors of the same objects.[49]

But although the argument *against* color objectivism that we are now considering depends upon a certain way of thinking about perception, *responding* to that argument does not depend on any particular theory of perception. Let us assume, for argument's sake, not only that a representational theory of perception is true, but also that any variation in color experience counts as a difference in which color is represented. Let us assume, too, that there is considerable perceptual variation and on many such occasions we have no way to determine which experiences are veridical and which are not. Granting all of that, for the sake of argument, why think that color objectivism requires that we be able to determine which experiences are veridical, especially now that we know how to determine whether two objects have the same or different determinate colors?

---

[49] See Kalderon (2007 and 2011) for such a view.

Let's look again at the thought experiment introduced by Byrne and Hilbert, those intelligent thermometers that we encountered earlier. Thermoms, recall, are calibrated slightly differently, and so where some register 70 degrees, others register 69, and yet others 71, and so forth. According to Byrne and Hilbert, even if Thermoms have no reason to believe that the temperature is exactly 70 degrees, they have good reason to believe that the temperature is around 70 degrees. Furthermore, even if they have no way to determine which among them are getting it exactly right, they have good reason to conclude that some among them are, and some of them are not.

Byrne and Hilbert might be right about Thermoms. And the same may be true for us with respect to colors. Certainly, there is a gap between there being a fact of the matter about who is correct, on the one hand, and our having a way to determine who is correct, on the other. But if our focus is on whether colors are objective features of the world, and not on salvaging some theory of color perception, we see little reason to care whether Byrne and Hilbert are right about Thermoms or us. It is reasonable to think that Thermoms will agree about whether it is about 70 degrees (whatever 70-Thermom degrees comes to), that they are correct about that, and that what they are correct about is an objective feature of their world. But although there may be a story about which of our intelligent thermometers is calibrated correctly, perhaps there is no fact of the matter. Certainly, if their measurements were in Kelvin (or Fahrenheit, or Celsius, or Rankine, or Réaumur, etc.), then there would be a fact of the matter about who among our Thermoms is correct. But all we know is that their measurements are in Thermom-units, and no reason to assume thus far that there is a precisely right way to be calibrated for that.

As things stand for Thermoms and temperature, things stand for us and colors. We generally agree about the colors of things, more or less, but not precisely. And although there may be a fact of the matter about who among us are calibrated correctly, we cannot assume that there is. But the reason this seems to matter for the objectivity of colors is that we have assumed that for there to be a fact of the matter about what color something has, there must be a fact of matter about which experiences are veridical and which not. We do not assume that for temperature to be objective there must be a fact of the matter as to how exactly it is veridically perceived. Why think otherwise for colors? The reason, we suspect, is that we have assumed that that is the only way to visually determine an object's color. We have conflated the task of individuating colors (of, e.g., determining whether two objects are colored the same or differently by *matching* them against the same background and under various lighting conditions) with the task of identifying the color that we have individuated (of, e.g., orienting a color chart so that unique blue is *located* in the "right" spot). The former task does not require that we specify ideal observers and lighting conditions; the latter seemingly does.

It is worth noting that Thermoms are not only analogous to us with respect to color experience, but with respect to our experiences of temperature as well. If the water in the pool feels cool to Michael, it will certainly feel cold to Jody, Jody being more cold-natured than Michael. Let us assume, again for the sake of argument, that these experiences are representationally different. Michael represents the water as cool. Jody represents the water as cold. Let us assume, too, that at least one of us is mistaken (the water cannot be both merely cool and cold after all!) and that we have no way to know who is mistaken and who is not. What is certainly true, however, is that Michael and Jody are both experiencing the water's temperature. And since we have a way to discriminate differences in temperature, we *can* make scientific sense of what it is that we are experiencing, even if we have no idea how *what* we are experiencing *should* be experienced.

Jonathan Cohen claims that our intuitions concerning temperature and color are importantly different. We find them very much the same, and we are now positioned to explain why. According to Cohen, where our experiences of temperature vary, it is plausible to think that some of our experiences are veridical and others not. But

> what makes the epistemic diagnosis attractive in the temperature case is the widely held (and true) belief that a temperature property such as *being 70°F* has a natural essence ... ; that is, there is a representation-independent essence for this temperature property that serves as a truth-maker ... of the conflicting representations ... But it is doubtful that we are equally committed to the existence of a representation-independent essence of *being red* that could serve as a truth-maker ... of conflicting perceptual representations" (50–51).[50]

The passage from Cohen nicely brings into focus the point that we wish to make, and the confusion that we have been at pains to uncover. We are certainly committed to there being an objective feature that we are experiencing when we experience temperature, but there is no such commitment to there being a fact of the matter about which experiences are veridical concerning the water's *being tepid*, much less its *being 70°F.* Indeed, we have no idea what it is to experientially represent the water as *being 70°F.* If we think of our experiences of temperature representationally, and if we think that those experiences represent

---

[50] Traditionally, kind essentialism holds that, necessarily, all and only members of a kind have the "essence" of that kind, where "essence" is usually construed as a set of intrinsic properties. Essences also play a semantic role, viz., they determine semantic extension, as well as a causal/explanatory role, viz., they cause and explain why kinds have the nominal essences that they indeed have. For example, "having atomic number 79" is the essence of the kind "gold" and said essence causes and explains why gold is "shiny malleable yellow metal."

very specific temperatures, then we currently have no idea who is experiencing temperature veridically, and little reason to think that we ever will. Likewise, with colors. We know, we can determine visually, whether two objects have the same color, relative to various standards of sameness. We know how to individuate colors, and we are certainly committed to there being a scientific explanation of what it is that we are individuating. Nothing more is required of objectivism. Where our color experiences vary, and assuming that they are representational, we often do not know which experiences are veridical, nor do we always know how to determine which experiences are veridical, nor do we have any reason to think that we ever will. Nor should we care, at least where the objectivity of colors is concerned.[51]

4.2 The Problem of Perceptual Agreement

The view that we have argued for is consistent with a pluralism about determinable colors. Although we and bees see the same determinate colors, our color spaces are different. That very same determinate color that is yellow and that we see as yellow might also be a very different determinable color, and one that bees see. Indeed, consistent with our view, different "normal" human observers might be aware of different determinable colors. We will say more about how this might go in Section 4.3. But it is fair to ask, if we must be pluralists about determinable colors, why not be pluralists about determinate colors as well? Indeed, why not be relationalists about colors?

The first reason, of course, is that we provided an account of determinate colors that we find superior to other accounts. Our account requires that you abandon the tripartite conception of colors introduced in Section 1.2, at least as it is commonly thought about, and we showed in Section 3.3 that conception of colors is inadequate. Not only are there colors that other animals see that have no location in the color space imagined by that conception of colors, but there are also colors that we see and can visually discriminate that go missing on that conception. Second, by avoiding a pluralism about determinate colors, we capture what is intuitively right about the color incompatibility claim. Just as nothing can have two determinate lengths at the same time, just as nothing can have two determinate temperatures in the same location at the same time, nothing can have two determinate colors all over at the same time.[52] But finally, relationalism faces a challenge that we will now discuss: the problem of perceptual agreement.[53]

---

[51] Of course, we should care, we must care, if our project is to provide an account of perception.
[52] Assuming, roughly, the same frame of reference.
[53] This section borrows from Shech and Watkins (2023). We thank *The Croatian Journal of Philosophy* for their kind permission to reemploy that work here.

We generally agree about the more determinable colors of objects. Otherwise, color vocabulary would not have earned its keep. It is also widely recognized that human color vision is fairly constant allowing us to see an object's color as constant across a wide range of lighting conditions, or at least that our judgments about an object's color will generally remain consistent even while viewing that object across a wide range of lighting conditions. Objectivists about color, those holding that an object has its color independent of how it is experienced, often appeal to such agreements. But these are not the agreements about which we focus here. We focus, instead, on determinate shades. This may come as a surprise, since, as we have documented, different observers under different circumstances will experience the color of an object differently and will even, at times, make different judgments about the colors of objects.

To appreciate the perceptual agreement that we wish to focus upon, imagine someone tasked with matching the color of some paint. This task is common enough. If we have painted part of a room and find we do not have enough paint, or we are repairing a painting or a car, finding exactly the right color might be very tricky. It will not be enough, for instance, for the new paint to match the old only under some particular lighting condition. A match in color will require that any observer (or at least any observer we care about) under any lighting condition (or at least any lighting condition in which the object might be viewed) will not see a difference between the new paint and the old.

Now imagine that the task was successfully completed. The wall painted with the new paint matches the wall painted with the old paint. Enter Susan and John. Susan sees the walls as slightly more purple than blue; John sees the walls as slightly bluer than purple. That's our old nemesis, perceptual variation, briefly entering the stage. What Susan and John agree on, what they might verify by looking at the walls where they meet across a wide range of lighting conditions, is that the two walls are the same determinate color. Indeed, a necessary condition for two objects having *exactly* the same determinate color is that no one can visually detect a color difference between those objects so long as those objects are viewed side by side and against the same background. (Of course, as we discussed earlier, even this might be insufficient for a perfect match, at least relative to very exact standards. Again, just as the standards for two objects having the same length might vary depending on purpose, so will the standards for two objects matching in color.)

It is important to be clear about what it is that Susan and John agree about. It is not that Susan and John agree about what color the walls are. They need not agree, in other words, on where they *locate* the colors of the walls. Rather, what they agree on, what they might well have determined visually across a range of lighting conditions, is that the walls *match* in color.[54] That is what Susan and John visually determine, not by seeing the walls at any particular moment, but over a range of lighting conditions. Moreover, when Susan claims that the two walls match in color, she is not merely claiming that they match for her, or for her at the moment. Susan's claim commits her to its being the case that the walls match for everyone (or everyone relevant to the standard she is using) across all lighting conditions (or every relevant condition for the standard she is using).[55] A nonobjectivist about color must, of course, explain how we often agree in our judgments about an object's color and why color language seems to ascribe objective properties to objects, and some have taken on that task (e.g., Cohen (2009) and Berit Brogaard (2015)). Their success or failure is not relevant here, however. Our interest here is not in how we might explain agreement in judgment. Our interest is in how to explain a particular kind of visual success: our ability to visually recognize and to agree that two objects match in color; our ability to determine that two objects are indiscernible in color across various lighting conditions.

What it is for two objects to look alike is simply for them to be visually indistinguishable, and so what it is for two objects to look alike in color is for their colors to be visually indistinguishable. Of course, once again, two objects might look alike in color under some lighting condition and not another. Or they might look to be different colors while against different backgrounds, but the same against the same background. But we assume that the commonsense standard for visually determining whether two objects have the same color is by looking at them side by side, against the same background, and under various lighting conditions. Susan and John, employing this commonsense standard, agree that the two walls look to have the same color. And we can well imagine that Susan and John are not alone. We can well imagine that no one could see a difference in color between the two walls. The two walls appear to be (at least very nearly) a perfect match in color. Everyone agrees.

Hardin, recall, tells us that any objectivist about colors should agree that "it is normally possible to determine what color a thing has by looking at it" (2003, 191). Due to perceptual variation and our inability to select the favored

---

[54] Susan may only care, of course, about human observers (and so not care about ultraviolet shades) or only the lighting conditions that are typically available to homeowners, including sunlight. For Susan, it's likely enough that no difference can be seen; she only needs the walls to match, not perfectly, but perfectly relative to her particular interests.

[55] The predicate "is the same color as" thus seems to work much as "is the same height as". And if, for instance, Susan claims of one wall that it is blue, she commits to treating as blue anything that matches that wall in color across observers and lighting conditions. In this way, at least, "is blue" would seem governed much as "is tall." It seems not to ascribe a relative or "centered" property, as, perhaps, "is tasty" might. An opposing view is suggested by Andy Egan (2007) and endorsed by Brogaard (2015). Also see Cohen (2009).

observers and conditions, he argues that objectivism should be abandoned. But we now turn this argument on its head. Every eliminativist about color should agree that, since nothing is colored, no two things can be colored the same or differently. But it is normally possible to determine whether two things are differently colored or the same color by looking at them, at least over a range of lighting conditions, against the same background, and compared side by side. That is what Susan and John did. They determined that the two walls have the same color by looking at them. Susan and John visually determined that the walls are alike in color. For Hardin, this success is illusory. The two objects are not alike in color despite Susan and John seemingly seeing that they are and everyone else agreeing, and despite our having every reason to believe that those objects share physical properties that explain their agreement.

A relationalist like Cohen might seem better placed to account for agreement. For Cohen, recall, each object has many colors, but colors are highly relational features of objects. On Cohen's view, the color that you see an object as having in direct sunlight is not the same color that you see the object as having in shadow, and so you see a cup that is half shaded as having two colors. This, to many, is counterintuitive. The cup, many will insist, appears uniformly colored, but partly in shade. Cohen's reply is that, although you will see two different colors, your judgment that the cup is uniformly colored

> is not a judgment to the effect that the regions are occurrently manifesting a common color, but rather to the effect that the regions share a color that one of them is not occurrently manifesting. That is, the subject judges that, although the unlit region looks different (in respect of color) from the region in shadow, the two regions would look the same (in respect of color) were they both viewed under sunlight (2009, 56).

So, Cohen might claim that when Susan judges that the two walls are colored the same, what she is saying is just that the two walls have all and only the same colors. John agrees. Agreement explained.

But this will not do. For Cohen, Susan is claiming that the two walls share a set of relational properties. John is claiming that the two walls share an *entirely different* set of relational properties. On Cohen's account, when Susan and John each claim that the walls have the same color, they are making radically different claims.[56]

To illustrate how odd this situation is, let's look at a very different kind of case. Cohen tells us little about what it is for a property to be relational. He

---

[56] Again, this is not to say that John and Susan cannot agree on what to name the color of the wall. Cohen attempts to explain that agreement (2009, Chapter 2). But John and Susan also agree that the walls match in color; they determine as much perceptually. But what they are agreeing on, if Cohen is correct, is radically different than they would have supposed.

thinks that we can make do with paradigm examples like *being a sister* (2009, 8). Imagine now two detectives, Jake and Hank. Jake is hired by Evelyn, who is a sister of Laverne. Hank is hired by Laverne. Noah is the father of Evelyn and Laverne. Jake concludes that Katherine, Evelyn's ward, is Evelyn's sister; and that Patricia, Laverne's ward, is Laverne's sister. Hank concludes that Katherine is Evelyn's daughter, and that Patricia is Laverne's daughter. It turns out that both are correct since the incestuous Noah fathered both Katherine and Patricia. Of course, Jake and Hank agree that Katherine is related to Evelyn just as Patricia is related to Laverne. But their agreement is accidental. Jake and Hank are equally correct and equally in the dark, but about very different relations. That's *Chinatown*.

Cohen's account of colors puts Susan and John in positions like that of Jake and Hank. Susan and John agree, but not about what they thought they agreed about. But the case for Cohen is odder still, even if not nearly as disturbing. For not only do Susan and John agree that the walls share a color, but everyone does. And, presumably, what everyone agrees about is that the walls share a property in common. But it turns out, if Cohen is correct, no one (or hardly anyone) agrees about what it is that the walls have in common.[57] The objectivist, on the other hand, has an easy and commonsensical solution: the walls share a common property; namely, they have the same determinate color.

4.3 Determinate Colors and Their Determinables

In Section 3, we offered an account of how determinate colors can be visually discriminated without appeal to some notion of "normal" or "ideal" observers and conditions. In doing so, we have said little about the more determinable colors, those color properties, like being blue, about which we most commonly discourse. For that matter, we have said little about the more determinate determinable properties, like being periwinkle or being cobalt blue. Saying more about how determinates and determinables are metaphysically related would lead quickly to issues highly contested, and those are controversies that we need not engage here.[58] But we will offer a suggestion, a story about how things might go, if only to show how the account of colors offered thus far might be fleshed out to accommodate the more determinable colors.

---

[57] The problem seems more dire still for a relationalist like Chirimuuta (2015). For Chirimutta, unlike Cohen, colors are not properties of objects, but of perceptual events. So it is not clear that Chiriumutta can make sense of standing colors at all, much less what it would be to match colors, and less still what it could mean for Susan and John to see that two objects have exactly the same color property. See Cohen (2015) for more critical discussion of Chirimutta's adverbial account of colors.

[58] See Jessica Wilson (2021a) for an overview.

How, first, do we individuate properties, in general, and not just colors, in particular? How do we determine whether the same property has been instantiated again or whether, instead, a different property has been instantiated? One suggestion, made famous by Sydney Shoemaker (1980), is to individuate properties by their causal features.[59] The suggestion is to individuate properties by how something's having that property makes a causal difference. So, something has a particular property if and only if that thing has a set of conditional causal powers. For example, something has the property of being flammable just in case, in the presence of oxygen, it would ignite if it came into contact with sufficient heat.

When John and Susan visually determine that the two walls are the same determinate color, it is plausible to assume that the two walls share certain causal features in virtue of those walls having the same color property. They are such that they would match in color across a range of lighting conditions for creatures like John and Susan, and perhaps for creatures very different than John and Susan. Those walls will also reflect light in very much the same ways. Let D be the determinate color shared by the two walls. Anything having D, then, will have a set of causal powers in virtue of having D: They will be indiscernible in color when compared to any other objects having D when viewed pairwise against the same background and under the same lighting for creatures having particular visual systems (including those like John's and Susan's); they will have nearly the same reflectance profiles; and so forth.

If we think of any particular property as necessarily having a set of causal features, then it is natural to think that a determinate property has all of the causal features of any determinable property that it determines, and that any determinable property has a proper subset of the causal features of its determinate properties.[60] So here is a simple story to illustrate the picture we have in mind. Periwinkle and cobalt blue are determinates of the determinable blue. Anything that is periwinkle will be blue, but something might be blue and not be periwinkle. John's favorite color is periwinkle; Fran's favorite color is cobalt. Susan's favorite color is blue. Something's being periwinkle, then, is sufficient for it to be favored by John. Something's being cobalt is sufficient for it to be favored by Fran. As we might put it, anything that is periwinkle has the power to be favored by John. Anything that is cobalt has the power to be favored by Fran.

---

[59] Shoemaker's view is stronger, still. Shoemaker (1980) holds that properties necessarily have their causal features; for any two possible worlds, if they are causally the same, then they are propertied the same. One of us is sympathetic to Shoemaker's stronger position. In any case, our story only requires that it is nomologically necessary that properties and their causal contributions go hand in hand.

[60] The position was influenced by Yablo (1992). See Watkins (2002 and 2005) for a development of this view with respect to colors. Also see Shoemaker (2007) and Wilson (2021b).

Something's being blue is not sufficient for it be favored by John or Fran, although it is enough for Susan's favoring it.

Of course, something's being periwinkle or cobalt is sufficient for it to be favored by Susan. After all, if something is periwinkle or cobalt, then nothing more is required for it to be blue, and so to be favored by Susan. And so, if periwinkle is the only color favored by John, but anything blue is favored by Susan, then anything that is periwinkle will be favored by both Susan and John; if being blue is enough, then being periwinkle must be enough. Susan, however, will favor things that are not periwinkle, so long as they are blue.[61] Being periwinkle or being cobalt, we might say, contributes all of the causal powers contributed by being blue, whereas being blue contributes a proper subset of the causal powers contributed by being periwinkle or by being cobalt.

Now what we have claimed for determinate shades like periwinkle and cobalt holds equally for the ultimately determinate shades we discussed in Section 3.3. Let D be some ultimately determinate color. Any two objects having D will be indiscriminable in color for John or Susan or anyone else. Any two objects having D, then, will perfectly match in color. Let's assume, too, that anything having D will look blue to all normal observers under all normal conditions, where normal observers and normal conditions will be that range of observers and conditions that we ordinarily count as normal. "Normal" is, of course, vague, and covers a wide range of observers and conditions. Given these very broad standards, some things will appear blue to normal observers under normal conditions and not appear blue to other normal observers under normal conditions. We return to this concern in Section 4.4.

Given our assumptions, plausibly, an object having D will be blue, but not all blue objects will have D. There are other determinate ways in which something might be blue. And presumably, for some object having D, there is nothing that its being blue might be responsible for that its having D is not responsible for. Put another way, the property of being blue contributes a proper subset of the causal features contributed by having D.

Now let's suppose that another determinate color, E, is also a determinate of blue. D and E are different properties, according to Shoemaker, since anything having D and anything having E will be causally different. John and Susan cannot discriminate by color any two objects having D, against the same background and across a range of lighting conditions. Likewise, John and Susan cannot discriminate by color any two objects having E, against the same background and across a range of lighting conditions. They can, nonetheless, discriminate objects having D from those having E.

---

[61] This is, of course, merely a play on Stephen Yablo's (1992) example of Sophie.

D and E, although they have different causal features, share some of the same causal features. They are, let's imagine, both such that any object having D or E would look blue under daylight to all normal human observers. They would be favored by Susan, though perhaps not by John or Fran. The property of being blue, we might say, contributes a proper subset of those causal powers contributed by both D and E (and many other determinate colors). Indeed, on this picture of properties, D is a determinate of the determinable blue *because* (1) anything having D will contribute all of the causal powers contributed by that object's being blue, (2) being blue contributes a proper subset of the causal powers contributed by having D, and (3) something can have all of the causal features contributed by being blue (and so be blue) without having D (and so without having all of the causal features of D) (see Figure 7). Indeed, this is simply one way to satisfy Yablo's criteria for determination that we discussed in Section 1.6: P is a determinate of some property Q only if: necessarily, for all x, if x has P, then x has Q; and possibly, for some x, x has Q but lacks P.

Before moving on, we should note that the account above is offered only as way we might think of how determinates and determinables are related. But what is important about this account is only that whatever is essential to a determinate property's instantiation includes whatever is required of the determinable property's instantiation. Take, for instance, an abstract object about which causal features seem irrelevant. One way of having a polygonal

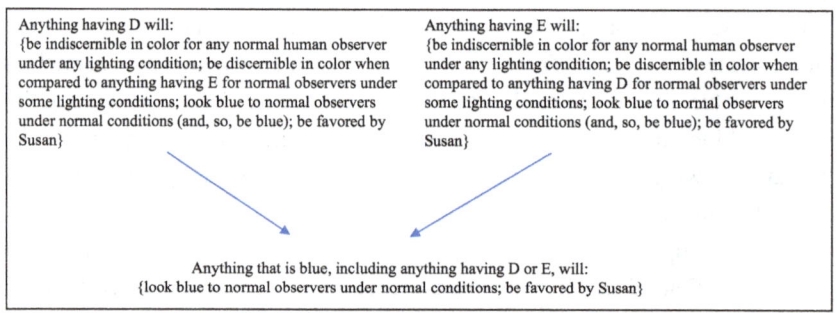

Figure 7 Determinates and determinables. Anything having the property D or E, as well as numerous other determinate colors, will be blue. What differentiates the properties D and E is that they do not contribute all and only the same causal features. What makes each a determinate of blueness is that an instantiation of either contributes all of the causal features of an instantiation of blueness, and an instantiation of blueness contributes a proper subset of the causal features of the instantiation of any determinate color that realizes it.

side is by being cubical; another is by being pyramidal. Something can have a polygonal side, then, and not be cubical. But anything that is cubical must have a polygonal side. Being cubical, then, is a determinate way of having a polygonal side, where having a polygonal side is a determinable both of being cubical and of being pyramidal.[62]

4.4 Objective Pluralism

In Section 1, we discussed various cases of perceptual variation. In Section 3, we argued that perceptual variation does not prevent us from visually discriminating the various determinate colors. What counts as being the same determinate color will be relative to a standard, just as being the same determinate length is relative to a standard. But, relative to whichever standard we choose, it will be an objective matter whether two things have the same determinate color.

It is no doubt true, however, that even if bees and humans see many of the same determinate colors, we see importantly different determinable colors. If we think again of the flower that looks uniformly yellow to us, but which appears to have two colors to the bee (see Figure 5), what are we to say about the flower's color? The flower has (at least) two determinate colors, one at its center and another outside its center, but intuitively it is uniformly yellow. This might seem to motivate relational or relative accounts of colors. For the objectivist about colors, however, the determinate color had by the middle part of the flower determines two different colors, one which the bee sees as different from the flower's outer color, and one which we see as the same as that determined by the outer part of the flower. The flower is both two different determinable colors, and the same determinable color, yellow. This pluralism, the fact that the flower's center has two different determinable colors, is explained not by a color's being a relational property, but by its having different

---

[62] It is worth noting that although the causal theory of property individuation and the subset theory of property realization are generally thought of together, the theories do different work and can come apart. Shoemaker has a causal account of property individuation (for the properties of concrete particulars), and he argues that it is an essential feature of such properties that they contribute the causal features that they contribute to anything that has them. The subset view is a theory of property realization; it is a theory about how the instantiation of a property realizes the instantiation of another. If you accept Shoemaker's account of property individuation, then a natural way to understand how one property realizes another is to claim that the realizer property contributes all of the causal powers contributed by the realized property, and the realized property contributes a proper subset of the causal powers contributed by the realizer property. But the subset view and the causal theory of properties are not essentially tied. The subset view merely holds that the realizer property contributes all that is required for the realized property, and the realized property contributes a proper part of what is contributed by the realizer property. So, for instance, the property of being pyramidal contributes everything that is required for having a polygonal side, and the property of having a polygonal side contributes a proper (and essential) part of what it is to be pyramidal.

objective determinable properties. And the explanation for why our experience is different than the bees is that our visual systems select for different (determinable) colors.[63]

But what of the fact that John and Susan, although they agree that the walls match in color, disagree about the determinable colors of the walls, and they disagree because their experiences differ? Either John and Susan each have veridical experiences, or at most one does, or neither does. Just how you answer that question will depend, in part, on what theory of perception you favor. Here we will be content to show that an objectivism about colors is compatible with a range of answers you might give concerning the experiences of John and Susan.

Let us concede first that Byrne and Hilbert might be right; perhaps there is a right way to be calibrated for human color vision. If that is so, then either John is seeing things rightly and Susan is not, or Susan is seeing things rightly and John is not, or neither is seeing things rightly. But we worry that there may be no fact of the matter about how best to be calibrated for human color vision, and we don't think that a verdict on color objectivism need be held captive to the answer to that question. As Kalderon (2007) suggests, just as the bees have visual systems that select for different determinable colors, perhaps John and Susan have visual systems that select for different determinable colors as well.[64] The objectivist might, in other words, be just as ecumenical about color vision as a relationalist like Cohen.[65] What the objectivist should insist on, however, is that nothing can have two ultimately determinate colors all over at the same time, just as nothing can have exactly two determinate lengths at the same time. That, it seems to us, is the color incompatibility claim worth saving.

4.5 From World, to Experience, to Language

We are agnostic about whether differences in color experiences are ever in conflict. We are agnostic, in other words, about whether color experiences are ever illusory.[66] We have attempted to remain neutral about how best to think about color perception, and partly to show that an objectivism about colors can

---

[63] See Kalderon (2007) for a development of such an account.
[64] Cohen (2009, 78–88) argues that relationalist accounts are superior to selectionist accounts, like Kalderon's. See Watkins and Shech (2022) for criticism of Cohen.
[65] Shoemaker (2003) offers another objectivist position that we do not take up. According to Shoemaker, John and Susan visually represent the same color but different appearance properties. Colors, for Shoemaker, are objective properties of objects, but a colored object also has very many relational appearance properties. We take our view of the (more) ultimately determinate colors to be compatible with Shoemaker's view of colors.
[66] See Kalderon (2011) and Watkins (2021) for arguments that there are no color illusions, at least if a color illusion is thought of as a visual misrepresentation.

be defended independent of any particular theory of perception. Color judgments, however, might seem a different matter. Plausibly, our ordinary color concepts are tied to how normal perceivers commonly see colors. The fact that normal humans under normal conditions see an object as red is surely part of the story about why "the object is red" is true. And now we seem to face the worry that we have tried earnestly to work around: How do we determine who the normal observers and normal conditions are?

Brian McLaughlin suggests, "as a first-pass," that we "appeal to our actual ordinary standards of normality, those we in fact tacitly invoke in everyday discourse" (2003, 482). It is important to note that McLaughlin's appeal to standards of normality concern color judgments, and we assume that something like McLaughlin's "first pass" is surely correct when we think about color judgments. It is because enough of us categorize objects as relevantly alike with respect to color that color language earns its keep. It is the reason that I can ask for someone to bring the red folder from my desk and reasonably hope that I will receive the folder that I desire.

Of course, worries about perceptual variation arise here as well. How many of us must agree, and under what range of conditions? But this is just the problem of vagueness, although not the vagueness that we typically think about with respect to colors. And, we assume, that whatever account of vagueness you hold, the sentence "the car is green" (uttered while pointing at a particular car) is either true or false (or partly true and partly false), and "it is true that the car is green" is either compatible with "it is true that the car is blue," or it is not. As it turns out, regardless of what you say, it is compatible with an objectivism about colors, as we will now show.

Thea and Sheldon disagree about the color of their car. Thea claims that the car is green (or at least more green than blue); Sheldon claims that the car is blue (or at least more blue than green). Perhaps, as Byrne and Hilbert suspect, there is an exactly right way to see the car, and then supposedly there is a fact of the matter about who is correct. Or perhaps, even if there is not a right way to see the color of the car, Sheldon is far enough outside the norm to count as abnormal. We need not say that he misperceives the color of the car, although we might. Color language is, however, our shared language. If Sheldon is far enough outside the norm, if normal perceivers judge that the car is not blue, then Sheldon's judgment is false regardless of what we say about visual experience. It will then be false that the car is blue. We might instead think that both Sheldon and Thea count as normal by our ordinary standards. It might be, then, that Sheldon and Thea are both correct about the color of the car, and that both are mistaken that the other is wrong. But we might also face cases where our ordinary color categories fail us, like with a surface whose appearance changes radically when viewed from different angles, or when viewed under different normal lighting. Perhaps, for some objects, there is no fact of the matter about whether it is blue or green. Every determinable color ascription will then fail.

Notice that, in outline at least, we have covered every possibility. Either Thea is right and Sheldon wrong, or vice versa; they are both right; they are both wrong. Our color language often succeeds; perhaps, at times, it overachieves; and perhaps it sometimes fails. Sometimes, perhaps, there will be no place to locate the color of an object.[67] Perhaps, at some determinable level, there is no determinable category under which the object's color falls, at least using the color vocabulary that we commonly employ. What we showed earlier, however, is that such an outcome does not threaten an objectivism about colors. An objectivist about color, qua objectivist about color, needn't care what we say about Sheldon and Thea.

5 Realism in the Metaphysics of Science

5.1 Colors in the World

We have argued for an objectivism about colors; objects are colored and have their colors independent of experience. That argument relies on our having provided criteria for identifying and individuating the ultimately determinate colors of objects. Nonetheless, it will seem to many a pyrrhic victory to have saved colors only to lose those determinable colors that we commonly discuss. To have colors, but to lose blue and red, will seem to many not to have saved colors at all. Section 4, and especially Section 4.3, suggested a way to think about the more determinable colors, and a way of understanding how the more determinable colors might be realized by those more determinate colors. Our suggestion is that, if we think of properties as being individuated by their causal features, then we have good reason to conclude that determinable colors are objective properties of objects. As we will see in Section 5.4, similar strategies are commonly employed in the philosophy of science.

In this section, we aim to show how objectivism about colors gains further support from recent work in the philosophy of mathematics and science, and especially in the context of biology. First, in Section 5.2, we discuss various realist disputes, particularly as they arise in the philosophy of mathematics and the philosophy of biology, showing how those disputes compare with disputes concerning colors. Second, in Section 5.3, we offer an alternative way of thinking about color space. There we show that our ordinary ways of thinking

---

[67] Gert (2006) argues that we can be realists about determinable colors without being realists about the unique shades. We agree with Gert, but we worry that the realist weakens her position, perhaps fatally, if she cannot defend a realism about ultimately determinate colors.

about color space can be understood as related to an enhanced color space much as our ordinary ways of thinking about the state of a dynamical system can be understood as related to phase space. Finally, in Section 5.4, we discuss recent attempts in the philosophy of science to explain how the entities and properties of the various special sciences "emerge" or are realized by underlying states of affairs. As we will show, those efforts mirror the way that determinable colors might be realized by determinate colors, as we suggested in Section 4. Our hope, too, is that the speculations that follow may engender interesting future work on such topics, and that it might forge fruitful connections between various areas of research.

5.2 Colors and Indispensability Arguments

To this point, we have mostly treated color objectivism as the default position. We have, at least implicitly, treated the position as the view everyone would have if they did not think they had compelling reasons to deny it. Consequently, our aim has been primarily to defend color objectivism against its many detractors. This is not to treat common sense as sacrosanct. But we all must begin where we are and, as it turns out, we commonly treat colors as objective properties regardless of what we think we ought to say while doing philosophy or science.

But even if we ignore common sense, even if we treat colors as purely theoretical properties whose status is prima facie up for grabs, a strong case can be made for color objectivism. For if we look at arguments in areas where common sense plays less of a role, if we look, for instance, at arguments for the objectivity of numbers or biological kinds, we find arguments fitted for our purposes.

Philosophers of mathematics, for instance, have long debated the ontological status of mathematical entities. Anti-realists hold that mathematical entities do not exist; or, at least, such "objects" don't have a mind-independent existence. Realists, or Platonists, argue otherwise. One realist line of argumentation, which is associated with Hillary Putnam (1971) and Willard Van Orman Quine (1981), concerns the Putnam–Quine indispensability argument, a main tenet of which is the Quinean ontic thesis that we are committed to the existence of any entity that we indispensably quantify over in our best scientific theories.[68] Due primarily to the work of Mark Colyvan (2001, 2007, 2010) and Alan Baker (2005, 2009, 2012), which emphasizes the importance of explanatory indispensability (instead of indispensability *tout court*), a more recent variant of the argument

---

[68] See Colyvan (2001) for an in-depth study of the indispensability argument and a defense.

has taken center stage in the debate. Here, then, is what Baker (2009, 6130) calls the enhanced indispensability argument:

(1) We ought rationally to believe in the existence of any entity that plays an indispensable explanatory role in our best scientific theories.
(2) Mathematical objects play an indispensable explanatory role in science.
(3) Hence, we ought rationally to believe in the existence of mathematical objects.

Accordingly, if we can identify indispensable explanatory roles of colors in science, then a similar realist argument might be employed for colors.

As stated, the indispensability argument is an argument strategy for defending a realism about objects, and not properties. But putting aside metaphysical questions about what properties are (whether they be universals, or tropes, or classes), properties or their kin play an essential role in explanations.[69] To be committed to numbers is be committed to some numbers being odd and others even, whatever metaphysical story you tell about being odd or even. To be committed to horses is to be committed to objects that are horses, and animals. In any case, for our purposes, if it is sometimes true that *two objects have the same color,* or that *some birds are colored*, and if what makes those propositions true is independent of experiences, then we have secured the objectivism about colors that we here care about. So, if appeals to colors as objective features of objects play an indispensable role in scientific explanations, and if we accept the force of such arguments, then we have reason to believe that objects are colored, and their having those colors are objective facts about our world.[70]

At the outset, however, we should distinguish between color as a topic of scientific investigation, that is color as an explanandum, and color as playing a causal or explanatory role, namely, color as part of the explanans of a scientific explanation. That color is a salient explanandum in scientific investigation is clear from studies into the physics of color and vision, and also from work in biology. For example, the phenomenon of color constancy (viz., the relative invariance of how an object's color appears despite changes in lighting and background) has been documented in many animals, and understanding the

---

[69] See David Lewis (1999) for further defense and explanation.
[70] There are two additional reasons to be suspicious of the indispensability argument as being only about objects. For one, the argument is meant to extract ontological commitments from our best sciences and so we cannot assume, a priori, that we will be committed to objects instead of, say, relations, events, patterns, structure, and so forth. Second, it isn't clear that at least some abstracta (like mathematical entities) are objects instead of properties or relations. For example, Shech (2019) argues that the fundamental group (the first homotopy group) of the configuration space of a two-dimensional electron gas system plays an indispensable role in explaining the fractional quantum Hall effect. But the fundamental group – in this case the Braid group – is more a property of the configuration space than it is an object of its own.

mechanisms that achieve color constancy in various animals is part of contemporary research (Cuthill 2017, 3). More generally, comprehending the evolution of coloration by, for instance, identifying the full range of evolutionary selection pressures acting on animal color patterns is part and parcel of the field of evolutionary biology.

What matters for the indispensability argument, however, is what serves as explanans, and there are reasons to believe that colors also play an indispensable explanatory role in biology.[71] For instance, Cuthill et al. (2017, 1) explains:

> Coloration mediates the relationship between an organism and its environment in important ways, including social signaling, antipredator defenses, parasitic exploitation, thermoregulation, and protection from ultraviolet light, microbes, and abrasion ... and measurements of color collected noninvasively and at a global scale are opening windows to evolutionary dynamics more generally ...

It is difficult to understand how coloration can achieve the previous tasks if colors are not real, mind-independent properties. For example, it has been argued that aposematism, which is the use of coloration in evolutionary interactions and processes, allows for both predatory avoidance and resource-gathering benefits, such as a wider foraging niche (Speed et al. 2010). Coloration here is playing a *causal* role insofar as it informs potential predators that an animal is poisonous or venomous and enables the expansion of an animal's niche. In fact, animals can exploit the fact that the same color pattern can be perceived differently by different perceivers; that some determinate color patterns will have different determinable colors based on perceivers. Some damselfish, for instance, possess ultraviolet face patterns that facilitate species discrimination and allow for a "secret communication channel" with, say, potential mates, while remaining largely hidden to predators insensitive to ultraviolet colors (Siebeck et al. 2010, 407). Notice that both determinate and determinable colors play an explanatory role in the story above. And notice, too, the fact that certain determinate colors determine more than one determinable color, and that they determine the particular determinable colors that they determine, also plays an explanatory role.

Similarly, consider the phenomenon of heightened diversity in community evolution, which concerns evolutionary interactions between organisms where the exchange of genetic information is minimal or absent (Ehrlich and Raven 1964). Biologists attempt to explain such heightened diversity. One idea, known as the "escape-and-radiate" hypothesis, holds that "the presence of repellent chemical defenses was proposed to open up an 'adaptive zone' of diverse

---

[71] Broackes (1997) defends a position much in line with what follows.

ecological opportunities and hence promote speciation by adaptive radiation" (Arbuckle and Speed 2015, 13597). In their recent study, Arbuckle and Speed (2015) argue that various defensive strategies in addition to chemical defenses, such as coloration, have effects on macroevolutionary patterns when both speciation and extinction are taken into account: "The effect of chemical defense is a net reduction in diversification compared with lineages without chemical defense. In contrast, acquisition of conspicuous coloration (often used as warning signals or in mimicry) is associated with heightened speciation rates but unchanged extinction rates" (13597). They also suggest that knowledge of defensive traits like coloration may have a bearing on the *predictability* of extinction. That colors facilitate novel prediction in this context further speaks for their status as objective properties.[72]

Another interesting example is the widely recognized fact that coloration is associated with individual condition and fitness in various animals. In a recent study, Hill et al. (2019) argue that plumage coloration signals mitochondrial function in house finches. For our purposes, we can set aside the details of what "mitochondrial function" consists of and emphasize that such a function is essential for cellular respiration and core respiratory processes that, in turn, affect the survival and reproduction of organisms.[73] Hill et al. (2019) also propose that mitochondrial activity directly controls carotenoid ketolation, which mediates the production of red ornamental coloration (see Figure 8). The idea is that birds with low mitochondrial function have limited ketolation capacity and produce yellow feathers, while birds with high mitochondrial function have improved ketolation capacity and produce red feathers (Hill et al. 2019, 3). An upshot of their study is a suggested solution to a fundamental puzzle in evolutionary and behavioral biology, namely, the question of "what maintains the honesty of signals of individual condition" (Weaver et al. 2017, 1). They explain (see Figure 8):

> Carotenoid coloration has been documented to signal a wide range of measures of individual performance, such as foraging ability, overwinter survival, immune system function, predator avoidance and cognition ... In turn, mitochondrial function is a critical component of these same processes. Linking the ornamentation used in mate choice to function of core respiratory processes provides a novel mechanistic explanation for why carotenoid coloration relates to a range of aspects of individual performance and why females use plumage redness as a key criterion in choosing mates. (Hill et al. 2019, 8)

---

[72] For instance, in the literature on scientific realism, selective realists like Psillos (1999) maintain that we ought to be ontologically committed to theoretical constituents that are essential for novel prediction.

[73] But see Heine and Shech (2024) and Heine and Shech (2021) for a philosophically friendly introduction to mitochondrial activity and performance.

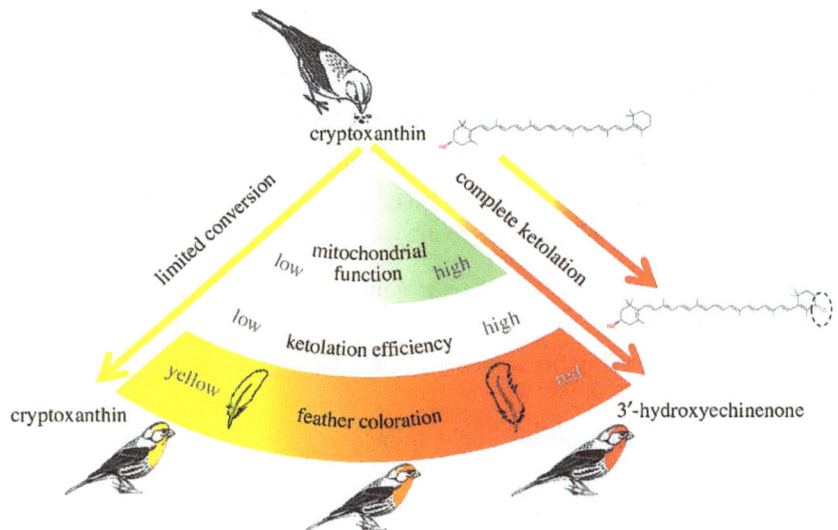

Figure 8 Coloration and mitochondrial function. Hypothesized links between red feather coloration and mitochondrial function. In order to produce red feathers, house finches ingest the yellow carotenoid cryptoxanthin and oxidize it to the red pigment 3-hydroxyechinenone. Ketolation efficiency, in turn, is linked to mitochondrial bioenergetics. (from Hill et al. 2019, 3).

The functional link between coloration and mitochondrial function, the task that coloration plays in evolutionary interactions and signaling, and the role of coloration in contributing to a possible solution to the above puzzle, all suggests that colors play causal and indispensable explanatory roles in evolutionary biology.

However, one may object that coloration does not satisfy the indispensability argument since – so the objection goes – it is possible to nominalize color away by appealing to other noncolor properties that supposedly carry the explanatory load. Accordingly, we wish to outline an argument that further solidifies the link between the role of color in biology and its metaphysical status. To do so, we need to say a little more about how biologist think about species and the relation of species concepts to mitochondrial function.

In particular, biologists have different ways of characterizing what constitutes a species. Such characterizations are known as "species concepts." One recent species concept makes a direct connection to mitochondrial function. Specifically, according to the "mitochondrial compatibility species concept" (MCSC), "*a species is a population that is genetically isolated from other populations by incompatibilities in uniquely coadapted* [mitochondrial and nuclear genes]" (Hill 2017, 397; original emphasis), and, "necessarily, organism O is a member of species S if and only if (iff) its (particular) [mitochondrial and nuclear genes] are uniquely coadapted to function well together . . . " to promote mitochondrial function such as cellular respiration and, thus, survival and reproduction (Heine and Shech 2024, 4). Importantly, biological taxonomies such as categorizing organisms into species (on various species concepts) play explanatory roles in biology. Thus, we have the following situation:

(P1) In some instances, coloration is a manifestation of mitochondrial performance.
(P2) Mitochondrial performance (via the MCSC) determines species membership.
(P3) Thus, in some instances, coloration plays a role in determining species membership.
(P4) Biological taxonomy, such as species determination, plays an indispensable explanatory role in biology.
(C) In some instances, coloration plays an indispensable explanatory role in biology (via its partial function in determining species membership).

If something along the lines of the above argument is cogent, then colors satisfy the indispensability argument, and this gives us independent reasons to hold that colors are objective properties.

However, one may object: Why can't colors be mind-dependent or even mental and still recover the proposed evolutionary value? For example, regarding the red plumage case, (a) the redness may be relational, or (b) the power to cause red experiences may be what is selected for (which is consistent with most color ontologies). The objection can be understood in two ways. One may grant that colors play an indispensable explanatory role but hold that this is consistent with relationalism or eliminativism. However, the conclusion of the enhanced indispensability argument isn't that something exists with qualification, for example, in relation to a mind, as an illusion of sorts. Rather, the claim is that if something is explanatorily indispensable to science, then it has an objective and mind-independent existence. The objector, then, presses the point: so much the worse for the indispensability argument. Still, this isn't the forum to offer a defense of the indispensability argument (but see Colyvan 2001 for a book-length treatment) and, in any case, the result is worthwhile emphasizing: a relationalist or an eliminativist about colors needs to reject the indispensability argument. For many this would be a weight too heavy to bear.

Alternatively, one may grant that the indispensability argument is sound, and then argue that colors don't play the necessary explanatory role. For instance, if mitochondrial performance is key for determining species membership, can't we nominalize away the role of coloration itself? In the philosophy of mathematics literature there are analogous attempts to nominalize away mathematics from explanations in science. But as Colyvan (2010) argues, "there is no easy road to nominalism." One must take the "hard road" and actually derive the sought-after result without appealing to mathematics. Such an approach is exemplified by the work of, for example, Hartry Field (2016). Analogously, if one wishes to take the hard road to nominalizing away colors from explanations in biology, one will need to show that the best explanation of various biological phenomenon can be had without appeal to coloration. For instance, if we reject the MCSC then the link to coloration is served in the context of biological taxonomy. This is an option open to the nonobjectivist, but it comes at a cost, viz., taking a stance on the topic of species concepts and rejecting the MCSC. Those reluctant to place constraints on science due to metaphysical considerations would not take such an approach.

One may retort, but other philosophers of science such as Atkins and Hahn (2014, 2015) and Chirimuuta (2015) have also looked at evolutionary biology and yet they have not concluded that it entails objectivism. For instance, Atkins and Hahn (2015) argue against the common assumption that human color vision evolved for seeing colors – what they dub "single use" theories – and instead suggest a spectral theory approach:

> [The] spectral theory does not deny the importance of environmental colour to the evolution of cone systems. . . . Undoubtedly, colour within the environment, both the statistical distribution of colour throughout the environment and the specific colours that are salient to human behaviour, is a large factor in any stable configuration of cone sensitivities accrued over time. What the spectral theory questions is whether a visual system needs to represent colours qua the reds, blues, and greens to make use of wavelength as a rich source of information. To this question, we answer not in general. (167)

What follows, for example, is that while "red–green perceptual pop-out may have been a contributing factor to the evolution of human vision . . .," "the explanation of pop-out need not be an explanation in terms of colour" (166–167). More generally, they hold that single use theories face a hurdle: "They must show that the capacity to represent the colours . . . was beneficial for some function, one that could not have been more easily performed by a chromatic and luminance contrast systems" (167).

In reply, first note that we are not claiming that evolutionary theory, generally speaking, implies objectivism. Rather, our claim is that if one can show that colors play an indispensable explanatory role in the explanation of some physical phenomenon, then one can apply the Indispensably Argument to reify colors. We then gesture at a particular phenomenon (coloration in house finches) and a specific theoretical framework (viz., mitonuclear ecology and the MCSC) that may do the trick. Second, on our reading, nothing in Atkins and Hahn (2015) is in direct tension with our discussion of coloration in house finches. For one, they admit that "colour within the environment" contributes to the evolution of human vision (and we're assuming the vision of house finches). For another, we agree with them that, in general, colors don't play a unique explanatory role. Instead, our claim is that, prima facie, by appealing to the MCSC, the specific case of coloration in house finches may fit the indispensability argument and we outlined other cases that may fit the bill as well. We don't deny that further work ought to be undertaken to substantiate the realist-objectivist case, but we submit that as much work needs to be done by our nominalist opponent. But here is a concession: if a realist-objectivist about color cannot display even one case of color playing an indispensable role in science, then, for many realist-leaning philosophers, the claim that colors are objective would be suspect.

Last, it is worthwhile to remind the reader of the dialectic structure of our argument. First, our primary argument for objectivism is in the sections leading up to this one. Our appeal to the indispensability argument is simply another route to what we take ourselves to have already shown and it thus further enhances the prospects for objectivism. Second, our goal in this section is to gesture at connections that may be made between recent literature in the philosophy of science and objectivism about colors. We are identifying avenues for potentially interesting further study. Whether these suggestions will bear fruit or lead to dead ends is a question that must be answered by future work.

5.3 Enhanced Color Space as Phase Space

We argued in Section 3 that there are more colors than there are points in the traditional three-dimensional representation of color space. That is, if our standards are very strict, if we require that objects match in color across all lighting conditions, perceivers, etc., including other types of animals, then we cannot locate the color of every object in the kind of color-space represented by Figure 1 (in Section 1.2). Moreover, as we noted in Section 4.4, the color spaces for different animals must be very different. And, as we saw in Section 5.2, those different color spaces, the different ways in which a determinate color might realize different determinable colors, play important explanatory roles in biology.

Abandoning the traditional three-dimensional representation of color space, however, might seem very much like abandoning the commonsense view of colors for which we have claimed to advocate. Surely that traditional

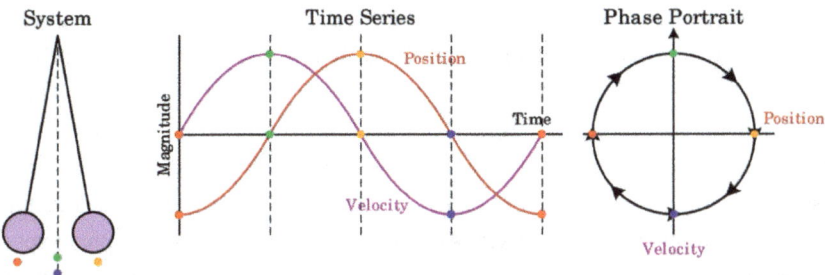

Figure 9 Phase spaces. Pendulum swinging from a small angle represented in various forms. From https://en.wikipedia.org/wiki/Phase_space#/media/File: Pendulum_phase_portrait_illustration.svg.

representation was on to something. We might, of course, claim that it represents only how colors look and not what they are, but the problem is that our experiences of colors are, well, experiences of colors.[74]

In this section we suggest an alternative way of thinking about color space, what we will call "enhanced color space." And we want to show how we might make sense of the traditional representation that we seem to have abandoned in relation to enhanced color space. To do so, we want to draw an analogy between color space and the dynamical system theory notion of a "phase space."

Consider systems of classical mechanics. For instance, if we consider a pendulum swinging with a very small angle in one direction, then there are two dynamical variables that describe the system: its position, r, and its velocity or momentum, p. Looking at Figure 9, the image on the left-hand side represents the system as it might be viewed visually, only in two dimensions. The middle image shows how the magnitude of both its position and its velocity/momentum variable oscillate. However, it is also possible to describe the state of the system with one point in a two-dimensional "phase space," where each point corresponds to the bob's position and velocity/momentum at a given time. Such a phase space representation is afforded by the rightmost image, the phase portrait.

Generalizing, the state of a classical system[75] of n point-like particles with six degrees of freedom (viz., three for position and three for momentum, with no internal rotation), which is confined to a volume V and energy E (like a gas in a box) is completely specified by a point $x = (r_1, p_1, \ldots, r_n, p_n,)$ in a $6n$ dimensional phase space Γ. Macroscopic systems, like a gas in a box, have particles

---

[74] This move would seem open to someone like Shoemaker (2003) who treats colors as objective properties of objects while treating color experiences as representing both colors and how those colors appear.
[75] See Goldstein et al. (2001) for overview.

on the order of 10^{23}, so Γ is typically a very high-dimensional space (e.g., in this case $6 * 10^{23}$ dimensions). Point x in phase space is referred to as the system's fine grained "microstate." In fact, x lies on a $6n - 1$ subspace of $\Gamma_{V,E} \subset \Gamma$. What is important to note for our purposes is that a microstate gives us the complete state of the system – it determines the values of all relevant variables – and that constraints (such as volume and energy constraints) reduce degrees of freedom and determine the relevant region of phase space. Additionally, a trajectory through phase space describes the dynamical evolution of a system, that is, the positions and momenta of all particles in the system through time.

Analogously, on our account of colors an ultimately determinate color corresponds to a microstate. Enhanced color space is a like phase space: it is a high-dimensional space that includes three dimensions for traditional color-space (like in Figure 1),[76] and additional dimensions for all possible lighting conditions, perceivers, and so forth – any variables that affect how a determinate color determines a determinable color at some place and time for some type of perceiver.[77] A microstate, or an ultimately determinate color, determines whether, say, Bob's car is cobalt at a particular time and place. If our standards aren't very strict, say, if we are interested in normal human observers under normal lighting conditions, this essentially introduces constraints – we are fixing possible perceivers and lighting conditions just like fixing a volume and energy for a classical mechanical system – that determines the relevant region of our enhanced color space (a subspace of the original larger space). In the limit in which we fix all relevant parameters and choose a "normal" human perceiver, the relevant region of color space will correspond to something like our traditional three-dimensional representation (such as Figure 1). A trajectory through an appropriately chosen sub-space may describe changes in lighting conditions, perceivers, etc. In sum, on our account all possible colors of an object are included in enhanced color space, but it is a high-dimensional space (like phase space). Discriminability of any two ultimately determinate colors will correspond to different points in enhanced color space.

Even if there are some disanalogies and lack of practical applications, appealing to a high-dimensional phase space can be conceptually useful. For example, it is well-known in the philosophy of biology that there are various notions of "fitness." One important notion that Abrams (2012, 8) argues is essential for natural selection is what he calls "parametric type fitness," a notion

---

[76] The dimensions of "traditional" color space likely needs to be indexed to the cognitive system involved since some animals may have corresponding color space with more than three dimensions (see Marshall and Arikawa 2014).
[77] Our high-dimensional color space may be countably or uncountably infinite.

of fitness that allows us to "view natural selection as a kind of process that can cause evolution." Here is how Abrams describes parametric fitness:

> We might view a population and its environment at a given time as represented by a point in a high-dimensional state space. This state space would represent the genotypes, phenotypes, locations, and internal physiological states of members of the population and of other organisms in the environment. It could also include the positions and states of abiotic elements that might affect survival and reproduction of members of the population. The state space would thus include all combinations of conditions which are relevant to the evolution of the population over the period of time under study ... We can then think of changes in the population and environment as a trajectory through this state space. Such a state space would be too complex to model in any detail, of course, but I believe the idea of it is conceptually useful ... For competing heritable types, the population at any one time will include a distribution of organisms with those types. Parametric fitnesses then summarize probabilities of possible trajectories through the state space: for example, trajectories in which higher-fitness types increase in frequency would be more probable. (Abrams 2012, 8–9)

In the same way that representing a population and its environment in a high-dimensional space can be conceptually useful in thinking about parametric type fitness, enhanced color space is similarly valuable for thinking about colors. The following section will partly showcase this point. Additionally, thinking about enhanced color space may help explain how the colors – as we humans commonly conceive those colors – fits into a larger scientific world view about colors considering the objectivism that we have defended. And once we see how colors as we ordinarily think about them can be thought of in relation to all of the colors, we find that this is akin to how other commonsense conceptions, such as motion, are commonly thought of within the context of a larger scientific conception of the world.

5.4 Scale-Relativity, Realization, and Emergence

In Section 3, we made a case for how the determinate colors might be individuated. In Section 4.3, we sketched an account of how determinate colors might give rise to various determinable colors. In other words, we sketched an account of how the fundamental colors – the ultimately determinate shades – might give rise to various non-fundamental colors. Similarly, in the philosophy of science, there is a debate regarding the metaphysical status of non-fundamental entities, from special science entities like house finches or viruses to the quasiparticles of non-fundamental physics such as phonons.[78] Steven French (2014), for example, defends

---

[78] A related issue is whether special science and other non-fundamental entities are (ontological or theoretically) reducible to the fundamental. Many holds that reduction implies eliminativism (Ney

eliminativism about non-fundamental entities, arguing that we ought only be ontologically committed to what is most fundamental.[79] In contrast, many philosophers of science hold that, in addition to the ontology of our most fundamental theories, we ought to believe in the existence of non-fundamental entities such as those appealed to by the special sciences. This view has been recently dubbed "rainforest realism" (Ross 2000), and one key issue concerns "the admittance criteria for the rainforest" such that "trout, viruses, phonons, and gases roam the rainforest," while "gerrymandered kinds such as trout-turkeys and concatenations of spacetime regions" do not (Franklin and Robertson 2021). Relatedly, various philosophers and scientists have suggested that matters of ontological commitment ought to take seriously the (spatial, temporal, and energetic) scale at which scientific phenomena of interest is manifested so that ontology is "scale-relative" (Ladyman and Ross 2007) or "scale dependent" (Shech and McGivern 2019). For example, in his review of effective field theory, physicist Howard Georgi (1993, 210) describes the situation as follows:

> One of the most astonishing things about the world in which we live is that there seems to be interesting physics at all scales. Whenever we look in a previously unexplored regime of distance, time, or energy, we find new physical phenomena. From the age of the universe, about 10^{18} sec, to the lifetime of a W or Z [boson], a few times 10^{-25} sec, in almost every regime we can identify physical phenomena worthy of study.

One manner by which to develop the idea that ontological matters are importantly related to scale is via Daniel Dennett's (1991) notion of a "real pattern": "a pattern exists in some data – is real – if there is a description of the data that is more efficient … " (1991, 34).[80] Ladyman and Ross (2007) modify and elaborate Dennett's theory:

> A real pattern is, very roughly, something that makes for a simplified description relative to some background ontology … For example, a wave on the beach is a real pattern to a surfer, or a lifeguard, because it is taken as the basis for prediction and explanation. Waves are very ephemeral real patterns, like currents and tides, but rocks and sandbanks are more durable. In physics, quasi-particles like phonons are taken to exist when their half-life is effectively infinite relative to the scale of the interactions that are being studied … Real patterns are entities of whatever ontological category that feature (non-redundantly) in projectible regularities (Ladyman 2018, 103–104).

2021). However, the views considered here assume that higher-level ontology is compatible with reduction (and so we don't enter here the debate regarding the viability of non-reductive physicalism).

[79] For French (2014) the fundamental ontology is one of structure instead of entities.

[80] Thinking of a feature or an entity as nothing more than a "real pattern" seems overly deflationary and instrumental. But this, for us, is a useful beginning. We hope to add more metaphysical muscle to the view as we proceed.

What Ladyman and Ross have in mind by "projectable regularities" is, roughly, counterfactual and nomological generalizations that are successful in explaining and predicting phenomena, while the notion of redundancy may be understood, for instance, in terms of information compression.

Recently, Vanessa Seifert (2023) has also suggested understanding Dennett's notion of an "efficient description" (and hence a real pattern) as a reduction in degrees of freedom (in that description). A "degree of freedom" here is understood as "an independent parameter needed to characterise an entity as being in a state functionally relevant to its law-governed properties and behaviour" (Wilson 2010, 281). Reflecting on how chemical bonds are treated in chemistry and in the philosophy of chemistry, Seifert notes that there is disagreement regarding what chemical bonds are and whether they truly exist (e.g., Hendry 2008, Zhao et al. 2019). Such disagreements stem partially from the fact that there are different methods for studying chemical bonds resulting in inequivalent characterizations.[81] In response, by appealing to the notion of an "efficient description" as a reduction of degrees of freedom, Seifert argues that chemical bonds are real patterns of interactions between subatomic particles (on any of the various characterizations of bonds).

Before continuing let us pause and reflect on the question of whether colors are scale-relative real patterns given what has been discussed up until this point. First, note that (at least) determinable colors are scale-relative. This is clear, for example, from phenomenon like Newton's disc, where a disc with seven colors (red, orange, yellow, green, blue, indigo, and violet) looks white while rotating. We can think of the rotation as a change in temporal scale that facilitates learning more about the various colors of the disc at different temporal scales. Additionally, a reduction in degrees of freedom typically corresponds to a change in scale so that when we constrain enhanced color space to (say) normal human observers and normal lighting conditions we are reducing degrees of freedom and essentially picking out scales of interest.

Second, if "a wave on the beach is a real pattern to a surfer, or a lifeguard, because it is taken as the basis for prediction and explanation" (Ladyman 2018, 103), then it seems that red feathers are real patterns for both house finches and the biologists who study them. Moreover, in the same way chemical bonds are real patterns of interactions between subatomic particles, it seems reasonable to think of colors as real patterns of interactions between light and other

---

[81] Seifert (2023, 273): "[If] we take ontologically literally what existing understandings of bonds state, then we arrive at the impossible result that the chemical bond is at the same time a *region* of high electron density (as per the covalent bond's definition), an *electrostatic attraction* (as per the ionic bond), *a form of association* between atoms (as per hydrogen bonds), and *the overlapping atomic wavefunction* (as per the [Valence Bond] approach)."

parameters in enhanced color space, especially as various determinable colors correspond to "more efficient" descriptions vis-à-vis a reduction of degrees of freedom in enhanced color space. Still, since these ideas are purely suggestive let us try to press the point a bit further.

In particular, a recent and related contribution by Franklin and Robertson (2021) holds that non-fundamental entities merit ontological commitment – reduction notwithstanding – when they are "emergent."[82] That is to say, such entities are admitted into the realist's rainforest via the criteria of emergence. Emergence, in turn, is characterized as follows: "An entity is emergent if and only if it is involved in [macro-]dependencies that are novel and screen off lower-level details" (7). We wish to inquire into whether colors are emergent in Franklin's and Robertson's sense so that they too be admitted into the realist's rainforest. To do so, we elaborate on the notion of "macrodependencies," and the conditions of "screening off" and being "novel." Starting with macrodependencies, which can operate at any scale but the scale of a putative fundamental theory, such dependencies can be dynamical or causal, and are often law-like. For example, a causal dependency is when "perception of predators by prey causes flight" (7). Similarly, when female house finches choose mates due to plumage redness, this concerns a causal macrodependency.

The screening off condition must satisfy dependence and independence parts. For instance,[83] consider a macrodependency where, under usual background conditions, water boils at 100°C. Let A be the boiling of the kettle and B the water temperature. Macrodependency B-A satisfies the dependence part of screening off because "water boiling depends on the underlying properties: the molecular motion of the water molecules is relevant to whether the kettle boils (if they are moving faster, then the kettle is more likely to boil)" (9). It also satisfies the independence part of screening off since "there are a range of distinct molecular motions that give rise to the kettle boiling – exactly how the boiling is realized doesn't matter" (9). But conditional on macrostate B (that the water is at 100°C), the molecular motion is irrelevant. And so macrodependency B-A satisfies the screening off condition. In other words, while there are many possible molecular motions, if the water's temperature is 100°C, then a set of molecular motions is determined that in turn guarantees that water will boil such that further details about the exact molecular motions are screened off.

Similarly, if we consider some macrodependency D-C where C is the selection of a house finch mate and subsequent evolutionary change via survival and

---

[82] Franklin and Robertson (2021, 4) argue that their "view encompasses that of Ladyman and Ross, but avoids some of the criticism levelled against their project."

[83] We follow Franklin and Robertson's example closely but, for simplicity's sake, we are leaving out a lot of technical details; see Franklin and Robertson (2021, 8–15).

reproduction, and D is plumage redness via carotenoid coloration, then we can see that screening off is also satisfied in two steps. First, since mitochondrial function or dysfunction is relevant for evolutionary success via survival and reproduction, it is thus relevant for mate choice. However, conditional on macrostate D (that a house finch has plumage redness), the exact details of the mitochondrial and nuclear genes at play and their interactions are irrelevant. Plumage redness determines that there is a high level of mitochondrial function (instead of, say, a dysfunction) such that further details about the mitochondria are screened off.

Next, is the condition of "novelty." A macrodependency, generally speaking, "is novel if and only if it's not type-identical to the microdependencies that instantiate it" (16). However, Franklin and Robertson note that novelty manifests in different guises in various sciences. In physics, the novelty condition is satisfied if and only if macrodependencies have a distinct functional form from the corresponding microdependencies. Returning to our boiling kettle example, novelty is satisfied since thermodynamics, the theory governing macrodependency B-A, is time-asymmetric, while the theory governing the microdynamics and thus microdependencies – classical or quantum statistical mechanics – is time symmetric. In short, this suffices to show that the functional form of such macrodependency is distinct from the underlying microdependencies.

In any case, the situation in biology is more of interest to our purposes. Franklin and Robertson (2021, 19) hold that in biology "a higher-level entity is novel if it has novel causal powers." They elaborate as follows:

> [Following Wilson (2011) and Takho (2020), the general idea] is that higher-level kinds feature a particular proper subset of the full range of causal powers located in the lower-level realising kinds. Novelty is then a consequence of the higher level having strictly fewer powers than its realisers. This guarantees that the higher level has a distinct but dependent causal profile. If an entity is individuated by its powers, then this characterization underwrites additions to the ontology. (18)

Their main example concerns Tabaco Mosaic viruses (TMV), which they take to be ontologically emergent and thus denizens in the realist's rainforest:[84]

---

[84] As for how viruses satisfy the screening off condition they explain:

> The dependency between a viral infection and, say, the mottling of tobacco leaves screens off the sub-parts of the virus. The presence of an active TMV will be sufficient to enable predictions regarding whether or not tobacco leaves will mottle or otherwise register signs of infection. As such, conditional on a property of the virus as a whole ... one can abstract away from any details of the state of the individual proteins that compose the virus, because the macrodependencies about the virus screen off these lower-level details. (Franklin and Robertson 2021, 23)

> In our view, where *A* [causally] depends on *B*, *B* may be understood to have the power or disposition to bring about *A*. The macrodependencies in which *B* participates determine what *B* can do, i.e. what powers has ... [Consider a macrodependency such that TMV (the "B")] have the power to mottle tobacco leaves [the "A"], [regardless of whatever particular amino acids happen to realize that virus]. So, the dependencies between TMV and tobacco leaves are distinct and of distinct types from the dependencies between the amino acids found in the leaves and the virus .... (18) [While virus-leaf dependencies] engender ontological divisions into plants and viruses, [protein and amino acid dependencies] engender much more fine-grained divisions into types of protein or amino acid, which can be found both in viruses and plants. (23)

Likewise, macrodependency D-C satisfies the novelty condition, where (*D*) plumage redness is causally related to (*C*) mate selection and subsequent evolutionary change via survival and reproduction in house finches. In particular, the mitochondrial genome of eukaryotes[85] contains only thirty-seven genes that code for thirteen mitochondrial proteins, twenty-two transfer RNAs,[86] and two ribosomal RNAs.[87] Further, there are approximately 1,500 nuclear-encoded proteins that function in the mitochondrion, of which, roughly 180 (call these N_O-mt genes) cofunction closely with mitochondrial genes (mt genes). Neither the individual genes nor the proteins and amino acids that compose the mitochondrial genome have the unique set of causal powers of plumage redness vis-à-vis mate selection, etc. It is through the efficient coadaptation and cofunction mitonuclear and nuclear genes – the mt and N_O-mt genes, and their interactions – that proper mitochondrial function emerges, which in turn realizes carotenoid coloration and thus plumage redness.

Given that macrodependency D-C satisfies screening off and novelty, it seems to follow that colors are ontological emergents that ought to be admitted into the realist's rainforest. However, one may object there is a disanalogy between Franklin and Robertson's emphasis on ostensible *entities* and *kinds* such as viruses and trouts as occupants of the realist's rainforest, and colors as *properties* of entities or objects. It isn't completely clear whether their realism is meant to extend to the properties of the objects in the rainforest. However, in macrodependency D-C it isn't that a house finch or its feathers are playing a prominent (causal) role. Rather it is plumage coloration that is salient, and this suggests that this case speaks in favor of admitting colors themselves into the rainforest. In any

---

[85] Eukaryotes are organisms whose cells contain membrane-bound organelles, including mitochondria, among other characteristics that differ from prokaryotes.
[86] Transfer RNAs (i.e., ribonucleic acids) transfer amino acids to ribosomes during the translation of proteins.
[87] Ribosomal RNAs aid in the synthesis of proteins during translation.

case, the general strategy being adopted by Franklin and Robertson, one according to which what is realized contributes a proper subset of the causal features contributed by whatever realizes it, was first employed to account for property realization and was later revised to account for entities and sortals.[88]

In sum, reflecting on Section 5.2, in some instances colors play indispensable explanatory roles in biology. Color space, in accordance with Section 5.3, ought to be conceptualized as high-dimensional phase space, what we called an "enhanced color space." Last, in relation to Section 5.4, determinable colors are scale-relative and it may be further reasonable to take them to be real patterns (perhaps of interactions of light and other parameters of enhanced color space), that are realized by those properties of objects that are responsible for such interactions, and so "emergent" properties that ought to be admitted into the realist's rainforest. Of course, we don't take our discussion in this section to be definitive, but we think it is suggestive enough to merit further study.

6 Conclusion

We see a world of colors because ours is a world of colors. That objects are colored explains why we see those objects as colored, and not the other way about. But although the world is colored as we see it to be, it is also colored in many ways in which we don't see it to be, and especially on any occasion of seeing.

Perceptual variation reveals to us that colors are perceptually complex, that a determinate color might well determine many determinable colors.[89] It does not reveal that colors are somehow subjective. It seems to only when we assume that identifying an object's color requires that we be able to visually categorize it, that we be able to properly locate an object's color in a simple three-dimensional color space. Once we realize that we visually discriminate the ultimately determinate colors by matching, the argument from perceptual variation loses its force. We can then solve the color problem without solving the color perception problem. And once we remember that our visual ability to match and discriminate determinate colors is a shared success, perceptual agreement, even amongst so much variation, lends further support for objectivism.

Exactly what we should say about the more determinable colors and the color judgments we make about them depends partly on which theory of perception wins the day, and about this we have attempted to remain neutral. We grant, at

---

[88] See Watkins (2002) for such an account of properties. Shoemaker (2007) develops a similar account and then shows how the account might be revised to accommodate individuals and the sortal properties they essentially have. See Wilson (2021b) for the most recent and most wide-ranging development of the general position.

[89] Watkins and Shech (2022) suggest that other properties and sense modalities are also perceptually complex.

least for the sake of argument, that there is no way to specify who the normal observers and viewing conditions are. We hold, instead, that once we are clear about how *arguments from perceptual variation* go, the objectivist has a reply that makes colors seem no more problematic than temperature or length. This, itself, puts us in the company of many other philosophers.[90] These philosophers have different responses to arguments from perceptual variation, mainly stemming from their different theories of perception, but they all agree that non-objectivism does not follow from those arguments. Remaining neutral about perception allowed us to canvas the range of replies available to the objectivist; we think this makes the case for objectivism even stronger.

Objectivism gains additional support when we look at how explanations in biology appeal to colors. Indeed, evolutionary success often depends not only on members of species having and recognizing various determinable colors, but often also on those determinable colors being determined in very specific ways. An animal might need to have both a determinable color easily recognized by members of its own species and a determinable color not so easily recognized by various predators. Only very specific determinate colors will suffice for having the different determinable colors that are required.

For some time, perceptual variation and the scientific image seemed to conspire against the view that colors are objective properties of objects. We hope that we have at least helped to level the playing ground.

---

[90] Indeed, it puts us in the company of every objectivist we have discussed (e.g., Byrne and Hilbert, Yablo, Kalderon, and Shoemaker).

References

Abrams, Marshall. 2012. "Measured, modeled, and causal conceptions of fitness," *Frontiers of Genetics*, 3, 1–12.

Akins, Kathleen and Hahn, Martin. 2014. "More than mere colouring: The role of spectral information in human vision," *British Journal of Philosophy of Science*, 65, 125–171.

Akins, Kathleen and Hahn, Martin. 2015. "Colour perception," in M. Matthen (ed.), *The Oxford Handbook of Philosophy of Perception*, Oxford: Oxford University Press, 422–440.

Albers, Josef. 2013. *Interaction of Color*, 50th Anniversary Edition. New Haven: Yale University Press.

Allen, Keith. 2009. "Being coloured and looking coloured," *Canadian Journal of Philosophy*, 39, 647–670.

Allen, Keith. 2016. *A Naïve Realist Theory of Colour*, Oxford: Oxford University Press.

Arbuckle, Kevin and Speed, Michael P. 2015. "Antipredator defenses predict diversification rates," *Procedings National Academy Science U.S.A.*, 112, 13597–13602.

Aristotle. 1941. "*De Anima*," J. A. Smith (trans), in Richard McKeon (ed.), *The Basic Works of Aristotle*, Modern Library: New York, 533–603.

Armstrong, David. 1969. "Colour realism and the argument from microscopes," in R. Brown and C. Rollins (eds.), *Contemporary Philosophy in Australia*, New York: Humanities Press, 301–323.

Austin, John L. 1962. *Sense and Sensibilia*, ed. G. J. Warnock, Oxford: Oxford University Press.

Averill, Keith. 1985. "Color and the anthropocentric problem," *Journal of Philosophy*, 82, 281–304.

Baker, Alan. 2005. "Are there genuine mathematical explanations of physical phenomena?" *Mind*, 114, 223–38.

Baker, Alan. 2009. "Mathematical explanation in science," *British Journal for the Philosophy of Science*, 60, 611–633.

Baker, Alan. 2012. "Science-driven mathematical explanation," *Mind*, 121, 243–267.

Bakewell, Charles. 1909. *Sourcebook in Ancient Philosophy*, New York: Charles Scribner's Sons.

Boghossian, Paul and Velleman, David. 1989. "Colour as a secondary quality," *Mind*, 98, 81–103.

Brian, McLaughlin. 2003. "The place of color in nature", in R. Mausfeld and D. Heyer (eds.), *Color Perception: Mind and the Physical World*, Oxford: Oxford University Press, 475–502.

Briggs, David. 2021. "Colour spaces," in D. Brown and F. Macpherson (eds.), *The Routledge Handbook of Colour*, London: Routledge, 140–156.

Broackes, Justin. 1997. "The autonomy of color," in A. Byrne and D. Hilbert (eds.), *Readings on Color: The Philosophy of Color*, Cambridge, MA: MIT Press, 191–225.

Brogaard, Berit. 2012. "Color eliminativism or color relativism?" *Philosophical Papers*, 41, 305–321.

Brogaard, Berit. 2015. "The self-locating property theory of color," *Minds and Machines*, 25, 133–147.

Brown, Derek. 2014. "Colour constancy and color layering," *Philosopher's Imprint*, 14, 1–31.

Brown, Derek. 2021. "Colour constancy," in D. Brown and F. Macpherson (eds.), *The Routledge Handbook of Colour*, London: Routledge, 269–284.

Burnyeat, Myles. 1979. "Conflicting appearance," *Proceedings of the British Academy*, 65, 69–111.

Byrne, Alex and Hilbert, David. 2004. "Hardin, Tye, and color physicalism," *Journal of Philosophy*, 101, 37–43.

Byrne, Alex and Hilbert, David. 2006. "Color primitivism," *Erkenntnis*, 66, 73–105.

Byrne, Alex and Hilbert, David. 2007. "Truest blue," *Analysis*, 67, 87–92.

Byrne, Alex and Hilbert, David. 2017. "Color relationalism and relativism," *Topics in Cognitive Science*, 9, 172–192.

Chalmers, David. 2006. "Perception and the fall from Eden," in T. Gendler and J. Hawthorne (eds.), *Perceptual Experience*, New York: Oxford University Press, 49–125.

Chirimuuta, Mazvitta. 2008. "Reflectance realism and colour constancy: What would count as scientific evidence for Hilbert's ontology of colour?" *Australasian Journal of Philosophy*, 86, 563–582.

Chirimuuta, Mazvitta. 2015. *Outside Color: Perceptual Science and the Puzzle of Color in Philosophy*, Cambridge, MA: MIT Press.

Christopher, Peacocke. 1984. "Colour Concepts and Colour Experience", Synthese, 58, 365–382.

Churchland, Paul. 2007. "On the reality (and diversity) of objective colors: How color-qualia space is a map of reflectance-profile space," *Philosophy of Science*, 74, 119–149.

Cohen, Jonathan. 2008. "Colour constancy as counterfactual," *Australasian Journal of Philosophy*, 86, 61–92.

References

Cohen, Jonathan. 2009. *The Red and the Real*. Oxford: Oxford University Press.

Cohen, Jonathan. 2015. "Outside color: Perceptual science and the puzzle of color in philosophy," *Notre Dame Philosophical Reviews*. https://ndpr.nd.edu/reviews/outside-color-perceptual-science-and-the-puzzle-of-color-in-philosophy/.

Cohen, Jonathan, Hardin, Clyde L., and McLaughlin, Brian. 2006. "True colours," *Analysis*, 66, 162–166.

Colin, McGinn. 1983. *The Subjective View: Secondary Qualities and Indexical Thoughts*. New York: Clarendon Press.

Colyvan, Mark. 2001. *The Indispensability of Mathematics*. New York: Oxford University Press.

Colyvan, Mark. 2007. "Mathematical recreation versus mathematical knowledge," in M. Leng, A. Paseau, & M. D. Potter (eds.), *Mathematical Knowledge*, Oxford: Oxford University Press, 109–122.

Colyvan, Mark. 2010. "There is no easy road to nominalism," *Mind*, 119, 285–306.

Cuthill, I Innes C., Allen, William, Arbuckle, Kevin et al. 2017. "The biology of color," *Science*, 357 (6350), 1–7. https://doi.org/10.1126/science.aan0221.

Deleniv, Sophia. 2015. "The mystery of tetrachromacy: If 12% of women have four cone types in their eyes, why do so few of them actually see more colors," *Neurosphere*. https://theneurospherecom.wordpress.com/2015/12/17/the-mystery-of-tetrachromacy-if-12-of-women-have-four-cone-types-in-their-eyes-why-do-so-few-of-them-actually-see-more-colours/.

Dennett, Daniel. 1991. "Real patterns," *The Journal of Philosophy*, 88, 27–51.

Descartes, Rene. 1644/1988. *Principles of Philosophy*, Blair Reynolds (trans.), Lewiston: E. Mellen Press.

Egan, Andy. 2007. "Secondary qualities and self-location," *Philosophy and Phenomenological Research*, 72, 97–119.

Ehrlich, Paul and Peter Raven. 1964. "Butterflies and plants: A study in coevolution", *The Society for the Study of Evolution*, 18, 586–608.

Field, Harty 2016. *Science without Numbers: A Defense of Nominalism*, Oxford: Oxford University Press.

Franklin, Alexander and Katie Robertson. 2021. "Emerging into the rainforest: Emergence and special science ontology." http://philsci-archive.pitt.edu/19912/.

French, Steven. 2014. *The Structure of the World*. Oxford: Oxford University Press.

Galileo. 1623. *The Assayer*, Stillman Drake (trans.), Stanford: Stanford University Press.

Georgi, Howard. 1993. "Effective field theory," *Annual Review of Nuclear and Particle Science*, 43, 209–252.

Gert, Joshua. 2006. "A realistic color realism," *Australasian Journal of Philosophy*, 84, 565–589.

Gert, Joshua. 2008. "What colors could not be: An argument for color primitivism," *Journal of Philosophy*, 105, 128–155.

Gert, Joshua. 2010. "Color constancy, complexity, and counterfactual," *Nous*, 44, 669–680.

Gert, Joshua. 2017. *Primitive Colors*. Oxford: Oxford University Press.

Gert, Joshua. 2021. "Primitivist objectivism," in D. Brown and F. Macpherson (eds.), *The Routledge Handbook of Colour*, London: Routledge, 299–310.

Gierlinger, Frederik and Westphal, Jonathan. 2021. "The logic of colour concepts," in D. Brown and F. Macpherson (eds.), *The Routledge Handbook of Colour*, London: Routledge, 81–90.

Goldstein, Hebert, Poole, Charles, and John Safko. 2001. *Classical Mechanics*. 3rd ed, Essex: Pearson.

Graham, Jody. 2002. "Room enough for one: Towards a solution for colour incompatibility," *Philosophical Investigations*, 22, 240–261.

Greenfieldboyce, Nell. 2014. "The X's are the same shade, so what does that say about color?" *National Public Radio*. www.npr.org/sections/health-shots/2014/11/10/361219912/if-the-same-shade-looks-both-yellow-and-gray-whats-color.

Hardin, Clyde L. 1988. *Color for Philosophers: Unweaving the Rainbow*. Indianapolis: Hackett.

Hardin, Clyde L. 2003. "A spectral reflectance doth not a color make," *Journal of Philosophy*, 100, 191–202.

Heine, Kyle B. and Elay Shech. 2021. "Roles of mitonuclear ecology and sex in conceptualizing evolutionary fitness," *Biology & Philosophy*, 36, 1–20.

Heine, Kyle B. and Elay Shech. 2024. "The mitonuclear compatibility species concept, intrinsic essentialism, and natural kinds," *Philosophy of Science*, 1–33. https://doi.org/10.1017/psa.2024.18.

Hendry, Robin. 2008. "Two conceptions of the chemical bond," *Philosophy of Science*, 75, 909–920.

Hering, Ewald. 1964. *Outlines of a Theory of the Light Sense*, L. M. Hurvich and D. Jameson (trans.), Cambridge, MA: Harvard University Press.

Hilbert, David. 1987. *Color and Color Perception: A Study in Anthropocentric Realism*, Stanford: CSLI Press.

Hilbert, David. 2005. "Colour constancy and the complexity of colour," *Philosophical Topics*, 33, 141–158.

Hilbert, David. 2011. "Constancy, content, and inference," in G. Hatfield and S. Allred (eds.), *Visual Experience, Cognition, and Constancy*, Oxford: Oxford University Press, 199–211.

Hill, Geoffrey E. 2017. "The mitonuclear compatibility species concept," *The Auk: Ornithological Advances*, *134*, 393–409.

Hill, Geoffrey E., Wendy, Hood, Zhiyuan, Ge et al. 2019. "Plumage redness signals mitochondrial function in the house finch," *Proceedings of the Royal Society B*, 286, 20191354. http://dx.doi.org/10.1098/rspb.2019.1354.

Hume, David. 1739/2000. *Treatise of Human Nature*, D. Norton and M. Norton (eds.), Oxford: Oxford University Press.

Hurvich, Leon M., Jameson, Dorothea, and Cohen, Joseph D. 1968. "The experimental determination of unique green in the spectrum," *Perceptual Psychophysics*, 4, 65–68.

Jacobs, Gerald. 1981. *Comparative Color Vision*, New York: Academic Press.

Johnston, Mark. 1992. "How to speak of the colors," *Philosophical Studies*, 68, 221–263.

Johnston, Mark. 1997. "Manifest kinds," *The Journal of Philosophy*, 94, 564–583.

Kalderon, Mark Eli. 2007. "Color pluralism," *Philosophical Review*, 116, 563–601.

Kalderon, Mark Eli. 2008. "Metamerism, constancy, and knowing which," *Mind*, 117, 935–971.

Kalderon, Mark Eli. 2011. "Color illusion," *Nous*, 45, 1–25.

Kalderon, Mark Eli. 2015. *Form without Matter: Empedocles and Aristotle on Color Perception*, Oxford: Oxford University Press.

Kalderon, Mark Eli. Forthcoming. "Color and the problem of perceptual presence," https://philpapers.org/archive/KALCAT-2.pdf.

Koenderink, Jan and van Doorn, Andrea. 2003. "Perspectives on colour space," in R. Mausfield and K. Heyer (eds.), *Colour Perception*, Oxford: Oxford University Press, 1–56.

Kripke, Saul. 1980. *Naming and Necessity*, Cambridge, MA: Harvard University Press.

Kuehni, Rolf. 2004. "Variability in unique hue selection: A surprising phenomenon," *Color Research and Application*, 29, 158–162.

Ladyman, James. 2018. "Scientific realism again," *Spontaneous Generations: A Journal for the History and Philosophy of Science*, 9, 99–107.

Ladyman, James and Ross, Don. 2007. *Every Thing Must Go: Metaphysics Naturalized*, Oxford: Oxford University Press. With David Spurrett and John Collier.

Lewis, David. 1999. "New work for a theory of universals," in D. Lewis (ed.), *Papers in Metaphysics and Epistemology*, Cambridge: Cambridge University Press, 8–55.

Locke, John. 1690/1996. *An Essay Concerning Human Understanding*, K. Winkler (ed.), Indianapolis: Hackett.

McLaughlin, Brian. 2021. "Colour, colour experience, and the mind-body problem," in D. Brown and F. Macpherson (eds.), *The Routlede Handbook of Colour*, London: Routledge, 25–41.

Marshall Justin and Arikawa, Kentaro. 2014. "Unconven colour vision", *Current Biology*, 22, R1150–R1154.

Marshall, Dan and Weatherson, Brian. 2018. "Intrinsic vs. extrinsic properties," *The Stanford Encyclopedia of Philosophy* (Spring Ed.), Edward N. Zalta (ed.), https://plato.stanford.edu/archives/spr2018/entries/intrinsic-extrinsic/.

Martin, Michael G. F. 2006. "On being alienated," in T. Gendler and J. Hawthorne (eds.), *Perceptual Experience*, Oxford: Oxford University Press, 354–410.

Matthen, Mohan. 2005. *Seeing, Doing, and Knowing: A Philosophical Theory of Sense Perception*, Oxford: Oxford University Press.

Matthen, Mohan. 2021. "Unique hues and colour experience," in D. Brown and F. Macpherson (eds.), *The Routledge Handbook of Colour*, London: Routledge, 159–174.

Maund, Barry. 1995. *Colors: Their Nature and Representation*. Cambridge: Cambridge University Press.

Maund, Barry. 2006. "The illusory theory of colours: An anti-realist theory," *Dialectica*, 60, 245–268.

Maund, Barry. 2022. "Color," *The Stanford Encyclopedia of Philosophy* (Spring Ed.), Edward N. Zalta (ed.), https://plato.stanford.edu/archives/spr2022/entries/color/.

Ney, Alyssa. 2021. "Reductionism," in J. Fieser and B. Dowden (eds.), *The Internet Encyclopedia of Philosophy*. https://iep.utm.edu/red-ism/.

Noë, Alva. 2004. *Action in Perception*. Cambridge, MA: MIT Press.

Osorio, Daniel and Vorobyev, Misha. 2008. "A review of the evolution of animal colour vision and visual communication signals," *Vision Research*, 48, 2042–2051.

Pautz, Adam. 2006. "Can the physicalist explain colour structure in terms of colour experience?" *Australasian Journal of Philosophy*, 84, 535–564.

Psillos, Stathis. 1999. *Scientific Realism: How Science Tracks Truth*. New York: Routledge.

Putnam, Hillary. 1971. *Philosophy of Logic*, New York: Harper.

Quine, Willard V. O. 1981. *Theories and Things*, Cambridge, MA: Harvard University Press.

Raffman, Diana. 2015. "Similarity spaces," in M. Matthen (ed.), *Oxford Handbook of the Philosophy of Perception*, Oxford: Oxford University Press, 679–693.

Reid, Thomas. 1764/1997. *An Inquiry into the Human Mind on the Principles of Common Sense*, Derek R. Brookes (ed.), University Park: Pennsylvania State University Press.

Ross, Don. 2000. "Rainforest realism: A Dennettian theory of existence," in D. Ross, A. Brook, and D. Thompson (eds.), *Dennett's Philosophy: A Comprehensive Assessment*, Cambridge, MA: MIT Press, 147–168.

Seifert, Vanessa. 2023. "The chemical bond is a real pattern", *Philosophy of Science*, 90, 268–287.

Sellars, Wilfrid. 1962. "Philosophy and the scientific image of man," in R. Colodny (ed.), *Frontiers of Science and Philosophy*, Pittsburgh: University of Pittsburgh Press, 35–78.

Shech, Elay and McGivern, Patrick. 2019. "Fundamentality, scale, and the fractional quantum hall effect," *Erkenntnis*, 86, 1411–1430. https://link.springer.com/article/10.1007/s10670-019-00161-y.

Shech, Elay and Watkins, Michael. 2023. "The problem of perceptual agreement," *The Croatian Journal of Philosophy*, 23, 133–138.

Shoemaker, Sydney. 1980. "Causality and properties," in P. Inwagen (ed.), *Time and Cause*, Dordrecht: Springer, 109–135.

Shoemaker, Sydney. 2003. "Content, character, and color," in E. Sosa and E. Villanueva (eds.), *Philosophical Issues*, 13, 253–278.

Shoemaker, Sydney. 2006. "On the way things appear," in T. Gendler and J. Hawthorne (eds.), *Perceptual Experience*, Oxford: Clarendon Press, 461–480.

Shoemaker, Sydney. 2007. *Physical Realization*, Oxford: Oxford University Press.

Siebeck, Ulrike E., Parker, Amira N., Sprenger, Dennis, Mäthger, Lydia M., and Wallis, Guy. 2010. "A species of reef fish that uses ultraviolet patterns for covert face recognition," *Current Biology*, 20, 407–410.

Smart, John. J. C. 1975. "On some criticisms of a physicalist theory of colors," in C. Cheng (ed.), *Philosophical Aspects of the Mind-Body Problem*, Honolulu: University Press of Hawaii, 54–63.

Speed, Michael P., Brockhurst, Michael A., and Ruxton, Graeme D. 2010. "The dual benefits of aposematism: Predator avoidance and enhanced resource collection," *Evolution*, 64, 1622–1633.

Tahko, Tuomas E. 2020. "Where do you get your protein? Or: biochemical realization," *The British Journal for the Philosophy of Science*, 71, 799–825.

Thoen, Hanne H., How, Martin J., Chiou, Tsyr-Huey, and Marshall, Justin. 2014. "A different form of color vision in Mantis Shrimp," *Science*, 343, 411–413.

Thompson, Evan. 1995. *Colour Vision: A Study in Cognitive Science and the Philosophy of Perception*, New York: Routledge.

Travis, Charles. 2013. "The silence of the senses," in C. Travis (ed.), *Perception: Essays after Frege*, Oxford: Oxford University Press, 59–94.

Tye, Michael. 2006. "The puzzle of true blue," *Analysis*, 66, 173–178.

Watkins, Michael. 1994. "Dispositionalism, ostension, and austerity," *Philosophical Studies*, 73, 55–86.

Watkins, Michael. 2002. *Rediscovering Colors: A Study in Pollyanna Realism*, Dordrecht: Kluwer.

Watkins, Michael. 2005. "Seeing red: The metaphysics of colours without the physics," *Australasian Journal of Philosophy*, 83, 33–52.

Watkins, Michael. 2010. "*A posteriori* primitivism," *Philosophical Studies*, 150, 123–137.

Watkins, Michael. 2021. "Colour illusion," in D. Brown and F. Macpherson (eds.), *The Routledge Handbook of Philosophy of Colour*, London: Routledge, 257–268.

Watkins, Michael and Shech, Elay. 2022. "Colors, perceptual variation, and science," *Erkenntnis*. https://doi.org/10.1007/s10670-022-00574-2.

Weaver Ryan J., Koch, Rebecca E., Hill, Geoffery E. 2017. "What maintains signal honesty in animal colour displays used in mate choice?" *Philosophical Transactions of the Royal Society B*, 372, 20160343. https://doi.org/10.1098/rstb.2016.0343.

Wilson, Jessica. 2010. "Non-reductive physicalism and degrees of freedom," *The British Journal for the Philosophy of Science*, 61, 279–311.

Wilson, Jessica. 2011. "Non-reductive realization and the powers-based subset strategy," *The Monist*, 94, 121–154.

Wilson, Jessica. 2013. "A determinable-based account of metaphysical indeterminacy," *Inquiry*, 56, 359–385.

Wilson, Jessica. 2021a. "Determinables and determinates," *The Stanford Encyclopedia of Philosophy* (Spring Ed.), Edward N. Zalta (ed.), https://plato.stanford.edu/archives/spr2021/entries/determinate-determinables/.

Wilson, Jessica. 2021b. *Metaphysical Emergence*, Oxford: Oxford University Press.

Yablo, Stephen. 1992. "Mental causation," *The Philosophical Review*, 101, 245–280.

Yablo, Stephen. 1995. "Singling out properties," *Philosophical Perspectives, 9, AI, Connectionism, and Philosophical Psychology*, 9, 477–502.

Zhao, Lili, Pan, Sudip, Holzmann, Nicole, Schwerdtfeger, Peter, and Frenking, Gernot. 2019. "Chemical bonding and bonding models of main-group compounds," *Chemical Reviews*, 119, 8781–8845.

For my parents, Orit and Aharon Shech, my sisters, Naharin and Nadine Shech, my wife, Isabel Shech, and darling little Paloma Shech, light of our lives.
Elay Shech

For Jody and Kate
Michael Watkins

Cambridge Elements

Metaphysics

Tuomas E. Tahko
University of Bristol

Tuomas E. Tahko is Professor of Metaphysics of Science at the University of Bristol, UK. Tahko specialises in contemporary analytic metaphysics, with an emphasis on methodological and epistemic issues: 'meta-metaphysics'. He also works at the interface of metaphysics and philosophy of science: 'metaphysics of science'. Tahko is the author of *Unity of Science* (Cambridge University Press, 2021, *Elements in Philosophy of Science*), *An Introduction to Metametaphysics* (Cambridge University Press, 2015), and editor of *Contemporary Aristotelian Metaphysics* (Cambridge University Press, 2012).

About the Series

This highly accessible series of Elements provides brief but comprehensive introductions to the most central topics in metaphysics. Many of the Elements also go into considerable depth, so the series will appeal to both students and academics. Some Elements bridge the gaps between metaphysics, philosophy of science, and epistemology.

Cambridge Elements

Metaphysics

Elements in the Series

Ontological Categories: A Methodological Guide
Katarina Perovic

Abstract Objects
David Liggins

Grounding, Fundamentality and Ultimate Explanations
Ricki Bliss

Metaphysics and the Sciences
Matteo Morganti

Teleology
Matthew Tugby

Modal Naturalism: Science and the Modal Facts
Amanda Bryant, Alastair Wilson

Metaphysics of Race
Kal H. Kalewold

Metaphysics of Causation
Max Kistler

The Metaphysics of Gender
E. Díaz León

Reduction, Emergence and the Metaphysics in Science
Carl Gillett

Social Ontology
Brian Epstein

The Metaphysics of Color
Michael Watkins and Elay Shech

A full series listing is available at: www.cambridge.org/EMPH

For EU product safety concerns, contact us at Calle de José Abascal, 56–1°, 28003 Madrid, Spain or eugpsr@cambridge.org.